SHE'S HIDING UNDER THE TABLE

One Woman's Life with Asperger's and Depression

Max Burke

Order this book online at www.trafford.com
or email orders@trafford.com

Most Trafford titles are also available at major online book retailers.

Cover by Joe Canzoneri

Print information available on the last page.

ISBN: 978-1-4907-8887-6 (sc)
ISBN: 978-1-4907-8889-0 (hc)
ISBN: 978-1-4907-8888-3 (e)

Library of Congress Control Number: 2018906225

Trafford rev. 05/24/2018

 www.trafford.com

North America & international
toll-free: 1 888 232 4444 (USA & Canada)
fax: 812 355 4082

ACKNOWLEDGMENTS

Thank you to my daughter for editing for content. Thank you to my son for helping me rename the people and places.

Thank you to my editor (L. F.) of two years for editing mostly for grammar and punctuation and a little for content and language. More than that, thank you for becoming a good friend.

Thank you to a certain person for editing the content while leading Charis Circle's Writing with Intent. Thank you to the regular participants of Writing with Intent while I was involved.

Thank you to my friends in Red Rock Cave, who met in the virtual online space and encouraged me to write the original stories that begin this book.

Thank you to all the folks at the publisher that worked with me.

Thank you to everybody who has waited years for this book. I hope the wait was worth it.

CONTENTS

Order of Stories for Medium Girl in Maroon

Order of Stories for Girl in Beige

Order of Stories for Young Woman in Blue

Order of Stories for Woman in Red

SHE'S HIDING UNDER THE TABLE: ONE WOMAN'S LIFE WITH ASPERGER'S AND DEPRESSION

Part One – The Little Girl In Red

LITTLE GIRL IN RED

There once was a little girl named Max (short for Maxine) who liked to wear red. She liked to wear red cotton shirts, red corduroy pants, red socks, and red Keds tennis shoes. Max tore off the blue plastic labels on the back of her sneakers because they were not red. The little girl's favorite days were when she could wear all her red clothes at once.

The little girl who liked to wear red did not use many words. She did not understand why the other people used so many words, when the sounds from the other people mouths hurt the little girl in red's ears. Max preferred to quietly meow like the tiny furry girl the daddy called, "that damn cat!" The little girl in red also liked to climb trees. The mama said that her daughter was part monkey. Max knew that the mama would not lie about such things. So she was part monkey and part cat.

When the little girl in red was three, her family moved to a brand new, brick, house in Raleigh, North Carolina. The house felt very large to Max. She didn't think she could remember how to get from her new bedroom to the kitchen, so the little girl in red took a red crayon and drew a line on the wall from her bedroom upstairs to the kitchen downstairs. She was pleased with herself for thinking of a solution to her problem. The mama did not find Max to be so clever. In fact, she did not seem to like the red crayon on the wall at all. The mama got very loud as she pointed to the wall and called to the daddy to come and look. This was not the first time the little girl in red was misunderstood by the grown-ups that were assigned to her. It certainly would not be the last.

BEDTIME MONSTERS

The little girl in red resigned herself to the monsters. The monsters were big bullies that poked and prodded and teased the whole night long.

"Hey, little girl," they said in their gruff prickly voices, "we're going to kidnap you and make you live under the bed with us."

The child awoke at midnight with one leg already sliding off the big-girl bed. The railing the daddy had installed failed to do its job. The monsters were winning again.

"Ha!" they snarled. "We've almost got you."

Like gravity, the monsters pulled her down to their hellish abode under her bed.

The little girl barely jumped clear of their clutches and raced down the hall in her Winnie-the-Pooh pajamas that covered her feet, not just her legs.

She did not consider crawling into the bed with the grown-ups, for touch from humans felt like burning and pinching on her skin. The thin skin of little girl in red left her no way to get physically close to other humans. And so she just stood there at the end of her parents' bed, in the dark, feeling alone as usual.

Eventually the mama sensed her daughter's presence and said, "Max, you are a big girl now. Go back to your big-girl bed."

Once again she returned to the monsters. It was like this a lot of nights.

When she got back to her room, the monsters taunted little Max, "See there, they don't care about you. You can't count on those grown-ups. But we are always here. We will never leave you. We are your monsters, and you are our little girl forever and ever."

HERNIA

Because the monsters woke the little girl in red a lot of nights, she ran down the hall to her parents' bedroom a lot. Unfortunately, they were on the second story of the house, and there was a staircase between Max's bedroom and her parents' bedroom. One evening, the little girl made a wrong turn and fell all the way down the steps.

"What the…" The daddy and the mama awoke to a bump, bump, bump sound.

"It's Max. She's fallen down the stairs," said the daddy.

"Go get the car. We need to go to the hospital," the mama said.

At the hospital the doctor said the little girl in red was born with an umbilical hernia and that when Max's body relaxed after she fell asleep each evening, the hernia was pinching her; thus, nightmares and night terrors woke her each night. The little girl in red needed an operation to repair the hernia, and that should be the end of the pinching and the end to the monsters. The mama and the daddy were relieved to hear this.

The night before the operation, Max and her parents checked in to the hospital. A nurse asked if the little girl in red wanted to go see the new babies. The nurse picked up Max and took her to the window where the babies were. The nurse said, "You aren't a baby any more. You are a big girl who is going to have a big girl operation tomorrow morning."

In the morning, the doctor scooped up the little girl in red into his arms and took her to surgery. The mama liked how kind the staff was to her daughter. Soon the operation was over, and Max had a big bandage that went around her tummy. The mama was worried that her daughter would tear out the operation because she was such an active child. The doctor said not to worry, that the pain would keep the little girl in red still. Sure enough Max walked stiff as a soldier with her bandages around her. She didn't feel like running or climbing trees.

The hernia repair healed the pinching, but the little girl in red still had nightmares and night terrors a lot of nights. The monsters still teased her.

PIRATE SHOPPING

The mama said, "We are going to buy you a dress."

I do not want one, thought Max. *I need protection on my legs for sword fights. I got to climb trees when the other pirates try to take over the territory. I do not need a dress.*

The mama looked for dresses anyway.

Oh! Oh! Look! Over here! Thought the little girl in red to the mama. She opened her mouth and said the rare words, "Over here Mama."(The little girl pointed to the boys' section.) She thought, *a coat for a Pirate Captain!* (It is a blue sailor coat with RED chief stripes on the sleeve.) *This is mine. Got to put it on. Who stole my pirate coat and put it in this store? Uh oh. The mama's coming.*

"You want that?' asked the mama.

It's mine. I am the captain of the pirates! Max nodded to the mama.

"Tell you what. I'll buy you the sailor coat, if you wear the sailor dress with it."

The sailor dress is not so bad. Sailors not as good as pirates. Pirates have swords. I am a pirate. A PIRATE CAPTAIN! Let's get out of here. I have digging to do. The gold is just waiting for me.

LITTLE CLAY BABY JESUS

Little clay baby Jesus lived at the little girl in red's house at Christmas time. The mama pulled him out of a cardboard box with a straw house and his little clay mama and little clay daddy. There was a little clay shepherd and two little clay sheep and three little clay wise men. The little daddy and the little mama wore blankets on their heads. Little baby Jesus had a blanket diaper, but he didn't have a shirt. Baby Jesus told Max that he was cold, and so she took him out of his straw bed and put him in her pocket. He was getting warm in the little girl in red's pocket. She knew this because she could feel him in her hand. Max wondered why the little mama and little daddy didn't take off their blankets from their heads and put them on their baby. She knew how baby Jesus felt. The mama and daddy at her house didn't know how to make her feel warm either. They thought that when the little girl in red screamed, she wanted them to go away. When Max grows up, she is going to put her blanket on her babies and they'll be warm.

The mama said, "Max, Where is baby Jesus? He needs to be in his bed."

The little girl in red pulled out little clay baby Jesus from her pocket. He was warm. She could tell because she could feel him in her hand. Max put Jesus in his little straw bed. *I love you baby Jesus*, thought the little girl in red. *Sweet dreams and good night.*

MY BOY AND THE TREE

(Max's older brother is named Peter, but she thought of him as "My Boy.")

My Boy, the mama, and Max walked to a neighbor's house. The neighbor had a big tree in the front yard. The little girl in red was very good at climbing trees. She was part monkey. The mama said so. Max knew that the mama would not lie to her. She climbed up the tree, and My Boy came with her. He was not as good as her at climbing trees. He was not part monkey. They climbed and climbed. The little girl in red was higher than she had ever been. She could see far. My Boy wanted to go higher. He climbed over Max and soon she couldn't see him.

She heard his voice come from the other side of the leaves. "Come on, Maxie! Climb up here to me. Don't be afraid." But monkeys are smart. She stayed right where she was. My Boy said, "Okay chicken, but I'm going to the very top."

She heard My Boy. He was moving again. He was moving even farther away from her. SNAP!!!!!!!! The little girl in red saw My Boy go by her eyes very fast. He was flying like Superman. Only he was flying down instead of up. Max scuttled down the tree to find My Boy. Onto the ground she jumped because she was part monkey. My Boy was asleep. He could not see the little girl in red.

The mama and the neighbor came running out of the house. They had seen and heard My Boy fall out of the tree.

An ambulance came with lights that hurt the little girl in red's eyes and the noise that hurt her ears. The mama gave Max to the neighbor she did not know very well. The neighbor took Max to the baby sitter. The baby sitter that the little girl in red knew was waiting for her. Max did not want the babysitter. She wanted My Boy. But he had gone away. Max went to bed missing My Boy.

The next morning My Boy was back. The little girl in red heard the mama on the phone say he was lucky. My Boy was being quiet like Max. He was usually full of words. *Is he mad at me?* Thought the little girl in red. *He does not look at me.* My Boy watched the pictures in the big electric box. My Boy called the pictures cartoons. Max sat next to My Boy, and he sat next to her. The little girl in red thought, *Do not take away My Boy again. I want him to stay with me forever.*

THE SHERIFF

The daddy got a job in a small town in Kentucky as a computer programmer near the caves that the town boasted. The mama became the librarian in the courthouse. The library was upstairs but the little girl in red's sheriff was downstairs at the end of the hall. She would run the length of the hall into his arms and he would lift her up and chuckle with delight. The four year old, little girl wouldn't let her parents pick her up like she let the sheriff. Hugs felt like burns and pinches most of the time. But the sheriff was so much fun she didn't care what he felt like.

One day the sheriff decided to tease Max by saying the small security vault was the prison cell for little girls. This frightened the little girl in red so much that she started to cry. The sheriff's secretary said in an angry voice that he shouldn't have scared Max, and he apologized over and over again.

When a big trial came to town, the little girl in red's mother told her not to bother the sheriff because he had important business. Max didn't see how there could be more important business than herself. When the mama saw that her daughter was missing, she went downstairs to look for her. She finally looked in the large courtroom, and there on the front row was the little girl in red, asleep on the sheriff's lap.

One day the mama took Max across the street to the dime store. She told the little girl in red to wait on the toy aisle, and she would be right back. The mama did not come right back, and Max got very worried. She looked and looked and could not find the mama in the store. So she left the store and crossed the street by herself and found the sheriff. The sheriff asked where the mama was. Soon they were all reunited, but the mama had a very worried look on her face.

The daddy's work contract came to an end after a year. That meant it was time to move to New York City. That was a long way from the sheriff. The sheriff gave the little girl a stuffed bunny, to pay her for all her good work. But the little girl in red didn't want the bunny. She wanted her sheriff.

FIFTH BIRTHDAY PARTY

In 1966, the little girl in red's Aunt Lydia met Max for the first time at the little girl's fifth birthday party. Max's family lived in an apartment just outside of New York City where her father worked in a skyscraper as a computer programmer. Her mother, an elementary school teacher, had invited some of the neighborhood children to the little girl in red's party. When Aunt Lydia arrived, there were children dashing about the home, but none of those children was the niece that she sought. After looking through most of the apartment, Aunt Lydia asked the mama the whereabouts of the birthday girl. The mama pointed to the dining room table, decorated with a birthday cloth, "She's hiding under the table." Max's aunt walked over to the table and lifted the cloth. Under the table she found a little girl with big brown eyes.

Aunt Lydia said matter-of-factly, "Hello, Max. I am your Aunt Lydia. You don't have to come out from under the table for me. You can enjoy the party in your own way. I just wanted to introduce myself." The aunt of the little girl in red let go of the tablecloth, and the child under the table was alone again.

And that is where she stayed most of the party. She avoided crowds then, and she avoids crowds now.

KINDERGARTEN

The little girl in red was the youngest and smallest in her kindergarten class. It was decided the children would mostly be allowed to free play and not have much structure. Max drowned in this supposed freedom. The older girls wanted the little girl in red to be their baby when they played house. Max didn't want to be a baby. She was not a baby. Why should she act like one? She found the game boring. The boys wouldn't let her near their cardboard brick structures. And so, the little girl in red wandered the room for hours and felt lonelier than ever. One girl asked Max to jump down the steps that connected two rooms. The little girl in red thought it sounded stupid but followed the other girl to the steps and watched as the girl jumped and then fell. The other girl tore a hole in her chin and had to go to the doctor. She didn't come back to kindergarten for a long time.

Every day Max begged the mama not to go to kindergarten. The mama said, "It's only half a day. You can survive that." Somehow it felt much longer. The mama was pregnant. Lila was born January 3rd and the mama stayed home with the baby after her birth. The little girl in red got to stay home too and take care of "My Baby." No more kindergarten.

TONSILS AND ADENOIDS

My Boy kept getting sick, and so the doctor suggested that his tonsils and adenoids be removed. As long as one child was getting the procedure the doctor suggested to go ahead and do the same on the little girl in red, for precautionary reasons. My Boy was seven and Max was five.

A friend suggested to the mama that the mama throw a party before the operations and collect gifts that the children could open every hour after surgery.

When it came time for surgery, My Boy was afraid, and so he went first to get it over with. He came back coughing up blood. It frightened the girl in red very much. The people who took Max to surgery were very nice, and by the time she got to the operating room, she was no longer scared. But after surgery, her ears hurt very much. The nurse would only let the little girl ice one ear at a time. This meant the left ear hurt when the right ear was being iced and vice versa. The little girl in red felt like she had been tricked. She did not want to open the presents the mama offered her every hour. My Boy liked opening the presents, but Max was beginning to not trust grown-ups.

MY BOY GETS BEAT UP

My Boy was very smart. He used big words just like the grown-ups. He liked to read the big books called in-sike-low-peed-ee-uhs. The little girl in red didn't read these books because she already knew everything she needed to know. My Boy got so excited about what he read in the big books that he wanted to tell everybody he knew. But everybody else did not love My Boy like Max, the daddy, and the mama. The little girl in red wanted to tell My Boy not to talk. She wanted him to be like her. But My Boy could not hear her thoughts.

My Boy told some big boys what he read in the big books. The big boys thought he was lying. Max thought, *BE QUIET!* My Boy did not give up. He never did when he was challenged. The big boys started punching My Boy. *No. No. No. No.*, thought the little girl in red. *Don't hurt My Boy.* They kept punching My Boy, and Max started to cry.

I have to save My Boy, thought the little girl in red. She ran home as fast as her legs would go. She ran and grabbed the daddy by the hand. The daddy saw that Max was crying, and so he followed her. When he saw My Boy, the daddy started to run. The little girl in red had never seen the daddy run before. He scooped up My Boy and took him in his arms back to the house. Blood came from My Boy's nose. The daddy and the mama worked on My Boy.

Max was standing in the corner. The little girl in red felt bad. She was not big enough to take care of My Boy.

WILD KITTENS

Grandmama Ema had wild kittens in the old shack next to her farmhouse. The little girl in red watched her put leftover lunch into the chipped enamel pan. She mixed in dry cat food, powdered milk, and rusty water. Her grandmother didn't talk much because this was important work. Grandmama Ema did important work like feeding wild kittens after each meal and cooking oatmeal for Max when she woke up in the morning. The grandmother carried the cat feast out the back screen door. The door squeaked at her. The little girl in red followed Grandmama Ema, but the grandmother waved at her granddaughter to stay back. Wild kittens don't like little girls, not even a little girl in red. Wild kittens only like grandmothers. Max sat on the cold concrete steps. Grandmama Ema crossed the yard, and she disappeared into the small one-room building that the grown-ups called the Old Kitchen. The little girl in red saw big kitty cats race across the yard when her grandmother talked in cat talk. Cat talk sounds like this: Here kitty kitty. In cat talk, "Here kitty kitty" means I love you. Max didn't see any wild kittens, but she knew that they were there. My Boy told her and My Boy doesn't lie about important things like kittens. The little girl in red grew tired of sitting on the steps, so she hid under the house and sat in the cool gray dirt. *I am a wild kitten,* she thought. *Grandmama Ema can't see me, but she knows that I am here.*

SWIMMING

When she was five and six, they tried to teach her to swim, but she sank. Max flunked 'guppies' at the YMCA two times before they gave up on her. Both the mama and the daddy were good swimmers and enjoyed the water. They would carry the little girl in red in their arms to the center of the pool but she whined and cried in terror of the deep water.

The summer before first grade, a kindergarten-aged neighbor, Titus asked her, to jump off the diving board with him. Something inside her gut protested, but she followed Titus anyway. Max jumped, and then she sank, and sank some more. The mama was talking with the other mamas and had no idea what was happening. In fact, other than Titus, nobody knew she was struggling to reach the surface, and Titus wasn't paying attention. The little girl in red was drowning, and Titus was already planning his next dive. When she finally burst the surface, she gasped for air but had no way to stay afloat. She began a rhythm of sinking and then bobbing to the water's top to gasp for air. Slowly, very slowly, Max was moving toward the side of the pool. But she was losing the battle. When she was near the side of the pool, she gave up and sank one last time. And then a hand reached in and pulled the little girl in red out. It was Titus' older brother. The mama had finally seen her and had also seen that Titus' brother was within arm's reach. She yelled at him, "Get her out! She can't swim." And with that one swift yank, she knew life instead of death. The mama fussed at her. What was she thinking? Max had no answer for the mama or herself. She didn't understand why she couldn't crack the mystery of deep water. Why wasn't it like shallow water? Why was drowning something that could happen to little girls?

FIRST GRADE

It was decided to put the little girl in red into first grade at age five instead of age six. Maybe school would increase her social skills and her vocabulary.

A lady called Miss Green put Max in something called a reading group. Miss Green was the first grade teacher. The little girl in red liked the children in the pictures of the book that the woman called Miss Green had put into her hand. Max liked to pretend she was playing with the girl in the book. The girl in the book was friendly like the aunt of the little girl in red. The little girl knew this because both her aunt and the girl in the book were named Lydia.

When it was the little girl in red's turn to read, the teacher said she knew that Max was smart and that she wanted her to tell the teacher about the children in the picture by reading the words at the bottom of the page.

The little girl in red hated words, but she hated the teacher and the other children looking at her worse than she hated the words on the page.

So Max opened her mouth and read her the sentence out loud, "Run, Lydia, run." And then the little girl in red looked out the window where the Mama-wind lived and she tuned out the teacher and the other children.

WET PANTS

One day in first grade Miss Green announced that she did not want to be interrupted with the reading group she would be leading in the back of the room. It was a different reading group from Max's. Miss Green said that if anybody needed to use the restroom, he or she did not have to raise his or her hand. Only the little girl in red did not hear Miss Green. She was tuned in to herself and not really paying attention to the world around her.

Halfway through the reading group Max realized she needed to use the restroom. So she raised her hand, and Miss Green ignored her. The little girl in red kept raising her hand, and soon she was crossing her legs. She was too old to wet her pants, but eventually, she just couldn't hold it any longer. And so she let go, and urine went all over her desk and onto the floor. Max hoped that if she was really quiet, nobody would see the yellow puddle.

But it wasn't long before the boy who sat behind her yelled out for everybody to hear, "Max wet her pants!"

Of course the little girl in red was terribly embarrassed.

Miss Green was her regular, kind self. She called Max's mother to bring the girl clean clothes. The little girl in red's mother was a school teacher who usually couldn't take off to help her daughter. But she came anyway and she came with clean clothes.

Miss Green gave Max a choice. She could stay at school or go home with her mother. The mama said she had taken the rest of the day off, and it was okay to go home.

The little girl in red was too ashamed to stay at school, so she went home with the mama. This felt like a reward. Max rarely got to spend an afternoon with her mother.

By the time My Boy got home, he had heard the news and said the little girl in red was so lucky to get to come home. Max agreed she was lucky to come home but she had paid a big price to be with the mama.

PRIMARY CHOIR

Max's family moved to North Carolina when she was five. They soon joined a Baptist Church. The mama wanted My Boy and Max to participate in everything offered to them. That included Sunday School in the morning, Sunbeams for children on Sunday night, Vacation Bible School in the summer, and primary choir on Wednesday afternoons.

The little girl in red didn't want to sing in a group. She didn't like being told what to do by the choir director. She tried to resist but eventually learned all the songs because they were repeated so many times. Anybody could have learned them. Week after week, Max went to primary choir. After a few months, it was time for the performance in robes in front of all the grown-ups. The choir director ordered all the children to look at her. But all the little girl in red could see was all those eyes on her. She sang the words to the songs, and the mama was happy. Max swore she would never sing again. But she sang in choirs every year all the way to early adulthood.

CANDY AND KITTENS

Penny got hit in the head with a golf club. She had to have operations to repair her skull. Penny was the youngest of Aunt June's six children and only one month older than the little girl in red. When Penny was well enough to play again, Max was sent to South Carolina to play with her cousin.

And play they did. They ran round and round in the tall, above ground, pool in the backyard. They petted all the fluffy kittens they could find basking in the cool shade. Ada Lynn, Penny's oldest sister, explained a product that could remove leg hair without using a razor. The little girls were in awe. Six year olds don't need to remove leg hair, but Ada Lynn said it all with such importance in her voice that the little girls stored the new information for another day.

Penny and Max picked blackberries for a pie that Aunt June made for supper. The briars grabbed the little girls like big monsters and made the little girls scream until Penny or the little girl in red freed her cousin.

With pennies, nickels, and dimes in their pockets, they walked up the street barefoot to get penny candies and cold bottled drinks. Penny drank a soda and Max preferred a chocolate drink. They played in the pool some more before shucking too much corn. After supper with fried squash, chicken and dumplings, and blackberry pie, the girls read their books from the library and fell asleep to the sound of the fan, as they batted a lone mosquito.

Tomorrow would be another day full of adventure. It was some of the best days of the little girl in red's life. She never wanted them to end.

THE SWORD FIGHTS

Sometimes the little girl in red did not understand that she could hurt herself or that she could hurt other people. This was true in the infamous Roman-Christian sword fights that took place at Aunt June's house when Max was six years old. The older boys came up with the idea to turn tobacco sticks into swords. The older boys would be the Romans who slaughter the younger children, who were deemed the Christians. Cousin Amanda wanted to be the empress and Marshal from up the street, the emperor. They would judge the fights. Amanda begged the little girl to be her pretend child. But Max didn't want to be a princess; she wanted to fight. Cousin Jason helped her nail a cross piece on the tobacco stick. Now she had a handle on her sword.

In the first round, the older boys won all but one fight, the one against the wild child who slung her tobacco stick wildly. Max didn't think about hurting anybody and hit the other stick with every ounce of energy she could muster in her tiny body. She kept swinging until her opponent dropped his stick. The tiniest Christian had won her first round. The fights continued in this way until the tiniest Christian and the largest Roman, Donny, Marshal's brother, met in the final round. Donny held his sword in one hand, like a great Roman should. But Max used both hands to chop and hit until she finally won the battle.

"She cheated by using both hands," complained Donny.

"Nobody said you had to use only one hand." Amanda took the little girl in red's side.

"Christians win!" announced Emperor Marshal.

And so there it was, the mystery that stood before them all. How did the smallest and youngest child present win the sword fights? A little girl, no less.

Perhaps she just didn't know her place in society. Instead of pretend princess she chose to be a champion sword fighter.

AUNT LYDIA'S HOUSE

After Max went to Aunt June's house, Aunt Lydia wanted the little girl in red to visit. Max was afraid of Aunt Lydia because, unlike the mama and Aunt June, Aunt Lydia was strict. The little girl in red asked if Cousin Penny could come, too. That was no problem.

The first thing Aunt Lydia did when they arrived at her house was show the little girls a flat dog house on the kitchen wall. There were little flat dogs that went in the dog house. Aunt Lydia explained that there was a dog assigned to each person in the house and that she had two extra for Max and Penny. "If you get in trouble with me," continued Aunt Lydia, "then your dog goes in the dog house." The little girl in red was scared. She would worry about that dog house for a long time.

The first night they had fish for supper. Max had never eaten fish, so she passed on it. Aunt Lydia said, "That's okay. When you get older, your taste buds will mature, and you will like all kinds of food." The little girl in red wondered if she was going to be put in the dog house. Her aunt didn't mention it.

On Saturday, Aunt Lydia assigned everybody a chore. Penny and Max were assigned to sweep the back patio. There was plenty of pine straw to keep the girls busy. Aunt Lydia had three children older than Penny and the little girl in red. Dan was the oldest and the most mischievous. He found his cousins finishing up their pine straw pile. He said to the little girls, "Do you think you can blow out a fire?"

"Sure," responded the cousins.

"Okay, let's see about that. Only you can't blow until I say so." Dan lit the pine straw with a match. He let the fire get going to a good size blaze and then said, "Okay, blow."

Penny and Max blew as hard as they could, but they couldn't blow out the fire.

"See," said Dan. "This is why you should never play with fire." Then Dan ran away.

Aunt Lydia saw the fire and yelled, "What are you girls doing?"

"Dan did it. He lit the fire," said the little girls.

"Dan!" screamed Aunt Lydia at the top of her lungs. She placed the little Dan dog in the dog house.

Later that day, they all went to the largest indoor pool Max had ever seen. It was very loud and hurt Max's ears. Aunt Lydia said all the girls had to wear bathing caps. This was a new idea for the little girl in red. She and Penny were not swimmers, so they played in the shallow part of the pool. It was great fun. Aunt Lydia's was not all dog house and work. It was fun, too.

CHEERLEADING

The little girl in red's parents thought that while My Boy was playing on a football team, she should also be kept busy. And so Max was signed up to cheer for My Boy's team. Cheerleading made no sense to the little girl in red. The reason it made no sense is that there didn't seem to be an object to the game. She could make sense of what My Boy was doing. He was supposed to either run the ball to the end zone or stop the ball from being run. But cheerleading didn't have an object like football. And the rhymes were a riddle to Max's brain. So there she stood like a dummy at cheerleading practice. The other girls thought she was slow in her mind. But the truth was she just couldn't get herself to listen to the silly phrases. She was given extra practice sessions away from the other girls, until she could do the moves, if not say all the words. To make things worse, the little girl in red was the smallest of the cheerleaders and, therefore, thrown in the air every third cheer. This was very frightening. But just like everything else, she didn't say anything to anyone about her misery. Max just kept moving to the cheers and getting tossed into the air.

The next year, My Boy played for a different team. The little girl in red was told the cheerleaders would get to wear toy guns with gun holsters. Wow! That sounded like fun. But the guns never appeared, and Max was stuck once again in her dilemma. Although there were some cute professional pictures made of the little girl in red and My Boy in their uniforms, only My Boy was having fun.

THE GOOD GIRL

My Baby stayed with the babysitter all day while the mama went to work with other children that made her happy. My Boy and the little girl in red went to the babysitter's house after school. When they got there, they went somewhere in the babysitter's car. She had something called errands. Errands meant eight children squished into the car real quick or they got smacked. Three kids sat in the way back of the old station wagon. The mama told the little girl in red, "Don't hit anyone younger than you." Max held onto her words, as if they were original stone tablets from God.

The babysitter's daughter decided to pick a fight with the little girl in red. The babysitter wasn't there to see. She had left the car and was doing her errands. My Boy saw it. Every kid in the car saw the babysitter's daughter hit Max. Thud. She hit the little girl in red in the face. Max's lip tasted tangy. The little girl in red just sat there. The baby sitter's daughter was bigger than Max, but she was YOUNGER than the little girl in red. Max knew she was that younger thing that the mama talked about because she was a smart girl. The little girl in red thought, *the mama said I couldn't hit anyone younger than me.* Bam. She hit Max again. My Boy pleaded, "Hit her back. Defend yourself. Don't just sit there, Maxie. This isn't like you. You can beat her up." *The mama said I wasn't allowed to hit anyone younger than me,* thought the little girl in red. Mama, I am being a good girl. Whack. There was spit on Max's face. My Boy's voice sounded like he was going to cry, "Come on! What's wrong with you?" The little girl in red's face was wet with sweat, tears, spit, and blood. Max thought, *Oh Mama, I am being so good.*

The babysitter came back to the car. "Stop hitting on her." She said to the little girl in red, "If you are stupid enough to just sit there, then you deserve what you get."

Rock, Rock. Rock the girl in red. I am good for the mama, thought Max. *My Boy is ashamed of me. He doesn't understand.*

The mama finally came to get her children. The mama was so tired. She had worked so hard. She put My Baby in the front seat. My Boy and the little girl in red climbed in the back seat. Nobody said anything. The mama would never know how good her daughter was. Poor Mama.

FLYING

I'm flying. I'm flying so high, thought the little girl in red. The swing was at the top of the hill. The more she pumped her feet, the higher her plane went. No one could stop her. The mama wasn't there. The babysitter was inside where she always was.

Here I go, thought Max. *I'm going to let go and fly so high. 1…2…3 Wheeee! I am really flying! I can fly! I am part bird.* Bump. "OUCH," cried the little girl in red. *The ground hurts but not enough to stop me from doing it again*, Max thought. The big kids are watching this time. *Go away. I can't fly when people are watching. It takes away my magic powers. I am supergirl. You can't tell it because I look like a plain little girl to you. Oh wow. I'm swinging so high again. Feels so good. Puts wind in my heart. Makes me feel free from all of you. O.K. I'm letting go again. What's that? My Boy is yelling to stop. Quit yelling. You are going to jinx me. 1…2…3 Wheee! Oh god it feels so good. Wait. Wait. Don't want to hit the ground again. I'll use my super strong arms to stop the ground from coming this time.* Snap! "AAAAAAHHHH! My arm! My arm!" *Make it stop hurting.*

The babysitter came outside. "She's faking. Everybody go play. Don't pay attention to her, and she'll shut up." She turned to the little girl in red. "You better hope you aren't hurt because your parents will be so mad!" She walked back into the air condition and left Max and her pain on the ground.

"It hurts so much," the little girl in red cried. My Boy cried too and said he was sorry he couldn't make it better. The mama finally came and had worried eyes. The daddy took Max to the emergency room. She got a cast. The doctor said, "No more flying." He didn't know that the little girl in red was magic. *I will fly again*, thought Max. *Just not in front of anybody.*

WAITING ON THE MAMA

The babysitter fed the children a snack before rushing them outside to play after school. The babysitter had four children of her own who weren't exactly kind. My Boy didn't care about all of this. He had a way of figuring out how to play with just about anybody. But Max didn't have

My Boy's gift of play. In the two years they went to the babysitter's, she was five to seven years of age, and she just didn't know how to connect with the other children. She wanted to see My Baby, but the babysitter kept Lila inside, where her oldest son watched her.

The children could have told their parents that the babysitter's house was a tough place for kids to survive. But they just didn't talk about things like that. The little girl didn't talk much anyway. My Boy talked about all kinds of adventures, but he didn't seem to mention what did and didn't happen at the babysitter's house, including the day he hit the babysitter's second son with a baseball bat.

In the meantime, Max missed the mama.

The little girl in red sat under the babysitter's mailbox and rocked herself as she said, "Mama is coming for me." She would chant this to herself over and over again, as if in doing so, the mama would hear her.

Eventually the mama would come, but she was tired from working all day. She would ask her daughter why she sat at the mailbox. Why didn't she play with the other children? Max had no answer for the mama. All she knew was the mama had come. She had been broken out of jail once again.

There came day when My Baby said the babysitter had pushed her, and Lila had to get multiple stitches in her chin. That was the last day they went to the babysitter. Their prison sentence was finally up.

KIDS' WORLD

The little girl in red thought of a place just for kids. *In kids' world every kid had a kid car. They already knew how to drive them because kids are smart. In kids' world, every kid had a tree house and an underground house to hide from grown-ups. There was candy at every corner and milkshakes downtown. There was a racetrack and ponies to ride. In kids' world everybody liked each other and everybody was happy. They didn't miss their parents because the kids could take care of themselves. In kids' world,* Max was free and everybody knew the real little girl in red. She wished she was always in kids' world.

LITTLE GIRL IN THE DARK

Where is the mama lady? thought the little girl in red. *Why doesn't she come to me? Daddy man, I am alone, and I need you tonight. Why can't you read my thoughts? I can read yours. There are sharks on the floor and monsters under the bed. Vultures and bats circle me and nip at my ears. I am so scared. I am so alone. What did I do wrong? Why am I left alone every night in the dark? Maybe I am an ugly little girl or maybe I am invisible. I am going to be so good, and then somebody will take care of me. Smiling moon, do you like me? Twinkling stars, will you love me? Winnie the Pooh, are you my friend? Curious George, can you hug me back? Oh, God, I will be so good if you answer me tonight. I am going to tap my leg on the bed. Please make me go to sleep when I get to ten taps. Otherwise, the vultures will hand me to the sharks and the sharks will hand my remains to the monsters under the bed, and I will be lost in another dimension forever. I am so afraid. (1) I am so afraid. (2) I am so afraid. (3) I am so afraid. (4) I am so afraid. (5) I am...*

"Goodnight little girl in red," said the moon.

"We love you little girl in red," whispered the stars.

"I am your friend tonight," smiled Winnie the Pooh.

"I like you," said Curious George. But the little girl in red was asleep and she didn't hear.

"I am sorry Max," said God. "I am sorry for the pain and the loneliness that can never be erased. I am sorry that you can barely talk to your own kind. I am sorry that you are trapped inside skin that hurts when it is touched. I am sorry you are alone in the dark and that you have nightmares the rest of your life. Here is a breeze through your window. It is my hand. I love you little girl in red."

UNDER THE BED

In the day time, sometimes the little girl in red would disappear all together. She would scoot under a bed and listen to the rhythm of her heart and the air being pushed in and out of her mouth. She loved the quiet that came with being underneath a large piece of furniture.

Sometimes other members of her family came into the room. Only they didn't know that she was there. They could not hear her heart beating or her lungs breathing.

She was invisible, a small ghost to everybody but herself. She didn't know why she was under the bed. It was just a place that called to her in a good way when the lights were on. Max didn't know why her parents didn't crawl under the bed too.

After she had been under the bed for some time, she felt a desperate longing. The little girl in red wanted somebody, anybody, to find her. But they didn't. Nobody thought to look down and see Max being very, very quiet.

Sometimes she would fall asleep under the bed. But most of the time, she scooted back out and tiptoed around the house until she had found the mama and the daddy. Sometimes they looked up from what they were doing. Most of the time, they never knew she was there. Even though she was no longer under the bed, she still felt invisible.

THE CAT AND THE DADDY

At age seven, little girl in red and the tiny furry girl were close. They liked to follow each other around and meow and growl. Sometimes when the cat growled, she scared Max. But most of the time, they growled together. The cat's name was Dilly, short for Dililah. Dilly was the same age as the little girl in red. So when Max was seven, so was the cat. Dilly had blue eyes and black and tan fur. She was a Siamese cat. Dilly was pretty sure she was the children's real mother. One time, the mama had to go to leave the house all of a sudden, and she asked the neighbor to look in on My Baby. When the neighbor went into the sleeping baby's room, Dilly stood up in the crib and started growling at the neighbor. Nobody was going to hurt the furry girl's baby.

One evening the daddy and My Boy were wrestling and tumbling on the floor of the living room. My Boy was laughing so hard that the little girl in red thought she wanted to rumble and tumble with the daddy, too.

"Me, too." She said.

So the daddy wrestled both children at the same time. My Boy kept laughing but Max got scared and started to cry.

Dilly leaped into action. Her girl was not going to cry if she could help it. Dilly BIT the daddy on the leg for making Max cry.

The daddy screamed out, and the mama laughed in disbelief. Dilly had won the wrestling match.

GRANDDADDY

When the little girl in red was seven, she sat next to her mother's father. He was sitting in a giant, leather rocker on a long screened-in porch in South Carolina. It was flat tobacco land, and her umpteen cousins were running around their towering fathers as if they were trees. It was Easter, and the women were in the kitchen, preparing the annual feast. The ancient glass on the farmhouse tinkled with each deliberate movement of the women. The granddaddy rocked slowly, his watchful eye on the clan he had helped to produce. They were a rainbow of beautiful moving colors on the front lawn. Max did not understand the commotion in the kitchen or in front of her. She was not a person of crowds.

The little girl in red wanted to understand the man next to her. He had holes in his shirt where his homemade cigarettes left their marks. He hummed and he grunted, and his eyes were of one who had put in his time. He did not look at his granddaughter, and she did not look at him, except for a few brief glances to make sure her chair rocked in time to his. They were one for a few minutes on that Easter day long ago. Both of them pulled at their starched collars.

Does he wish for his everyday clothes the way I do? Max wondered. *Do his pretty socks fall down around his ankles, too?* For just a moment, they were the rockers and they were the watchers, her gray old man and herself.

He died that next winter when the cold froze his tired old heart. She missed him and wondered, *with whom will I rock and watch the rest of my days. Where else will it be acceptable to not talk, to just sit and rock.*

DOING THE DISHES

The mama was raised on a farm in South Carolina. She was the fourth of six children. The daddy would drive his family from North Carolina to the mama's old home place. Mama's home had an old farmhouse that belonged to the mama's mama. Max's grandmother was called Grandmama Ema by her 20 grandchildren. Grandmama Ema's house was a magical place where aunts and uncles renamed the little girl in red, Maxie Taxie. Sometimes these relatives seemed to know Max better than she knew herself because they could tell her stories about herself that she could not remember. There were so many cousins running inside and outside the grandmother's house. There was always somebody to do something with so many personalities in one place.

As soon as Maxie Taxie's family arrived at Grandmama Ema's house, the little girl in red paired herself with Penny for play and work. Penny and Maxie Taxie were seven when they were first assigned to do the dishes after one of the meals.

When the girls looked into the kitchen, they saw a mountain of dishes. So the two cousins scrambled outside and hid under the old farmhouse. Their mamas called and called, but the girls did not budge. Finally, Maxie Taxie got tired of being a bad girl and ran back inside, where the dishes were still waiting for the little girls.

The little girl in red wanted to do the washing part because she liked bubbles. Lots and lots of bubbles. You can't have too many bubbles. Penny knew all about washing and rinsing dishes in the sink. She was an expert. Maxie Taxie was not an expert at washing the dishes in the sink because she had an electric dishwasher at her house. Penny said the rinse water had to be scalding hot, and so she ran steamy hot water. She told Maxie Taxie not to put her hand in the water. Penny also told her cousin to slip the soapy dishes into the hot, hot water when she was finished washing each piece. Penny pulled the dishes out of the rinse water with the metal grabbers that Grandma Ema used to turn the chicken over in the frying pan.

The two girls hadn't gotten too far with their jobs when Penny announced there were sharks on the floor, and the floor was really an ocean. She didn't want the sharks to eat them. So the two little girls made a bridge from the kitchen table to the sink with all the kitchen chairs. Then the two girls walked the dirty dishes from the table to the bubbly sink one by one across the bridge. Penny also climbed up on the counters and walked across them to put the dishes in the cupboards after she dried them.

"Watch out!" called Penny. "The sharks are jumping on the counter!"

Maxie Taxie leaped up on the counter next to her cousin. Whew. That was close.

"Oh, no!" pointed Penny. "There are alligators in the soapy water!"

Splash, splash, splash, went Maxie Taxie.

"O.K., the alligators went back down the drain," Penny announced in her authoritative voice.

"Hey!" came a voice from the kitchen door. It was Penny's mama, Max's Aunt June. "What are you two doing in here? Why haven't you finished the dishes? How did all that water get on the floor?"

"SHARKS!" the cousins yelled in unison.

Penny whined, "Mama, you are getting eaten by the sharks. Hurry up and get out before there is nothing left of you."

"O.K. I'm getting out. But you girls finish those dishes." Flap, flap, the door closed behind her.

"Let's get some ice cream," said Penny.

"Grandmama won't let us," replied Maxie Taxie.

"How will she know? She is asleep on the sofa." Penny always was the smart one. They sneaked onto the side porch between the kitchen and living room and creaked open the giant freezer.

"Hey, who is in my freezer?" called their grandmother's voice from the other room. Apparently, Grandmama Ema was smarter than two little girls put together.

Rats! thought Maxie Taxie. *This doing the dishes takes way too long. Why didn't the big people understand that the sharks and alligators don't like little girls in their kitchen? Little girls' work is never done.*

ICE CREAM

Uncle Oscar lived with Grandmama Ema. He was her youngest child and also Max's mother's younger brother. He drove his old truck to the front steps of Grandmama Ema's farmhouse. "Want some ice cream, Maxie Taxie and Penny Winnie?"

"Yes!" they screamed, while jumping up.

"Go get the other kids. We are leaving in ten minutes."

Cousins came running from every part of the house and yard. Soon Uncle Oscar's truck was full. Uncle Oscar drove to something he called "town." In the big city of North Carolina, the little girl in red didn't go to town, she just went to the store. In town, all the children picked out the kind of ice cream they wanted from the cooler in the tired old store.

Maxie Taxie did not want to talk to the stranger. She had never had to get ice cream like this. In Charlotte ice cream came out of a box in her home's freezer.

Uncle Oscar leaned over the little girl in red's back. "Maxie Taxie, do you know what flavor you want?"

Flavor! What does flavor mean? I just want ice cream, thought Max.

"Do you want vanilla?" asked Uncle Oscar.

"No."

"Do you want strawberry?"

"No."

"How about chocolate?"

"Yes, chocolate."

A chocolate ice cream cone was put in the little girl's hand. When she got out of the store and joined all her cousins, who were all licking their ice cream, Maxie Taxie's ice cream ball fell off her cone and onto the ground. Tears came to her eyes. She did not want to cry but she was.

"It's okay Maxie Taxie," came a voice behind her. It was Uncle Oscar, and he was not mad. "I will get you another one," he said, and he did. He sat down with his niece under the cool shade of an ancient tree with her new cone.

Everyone was eating his and her ice cream. Everyone was happy.

"Do you like your ice cream, Maxie Taxie?" asked her kind uncle.

"Yes." *And I like Uncle Oscar too.*

GRANDMAMA'S CHURCH

The little girl in red hid behind Grandmama Ema's stocky frame as they approached the concrete steps of the tiny Baptist Church. One of her thin socks, with lace on top, slipped down into her patent leather shoe. She preferred her gym socks and sneakers. But the grandmother took pride in her visiting kin. Max was bathed, brushed, buttoned, and buckled.

"Good morning, Mrs. Jones," yet another church member chirped, in respect to the woman who had been the adult Sunday School teacher forty years, "and who is this you have with you?"

A strong hand brought the little girl in red front and center. She could smell Grandmama Ema's mixture of baby powder, ivory soap, and sweat when she said, "Max, say hello so we can get to church on time."

Although the little girl in red heard the command, as usual, she was pretty sure her mouth had been glued shut. She tugged on her sock to no avail. Her grandmother cleared her throat and announced to the small gathering, "This is Max. She is Susan's middle child." With that, they marched up the steps and into the white clapboard building.

The little girl in red loved the smell of the worn pews. She was a city girl, used to the new city church building with the smell of new carpet and new seat cushions. She preferred the smell of the old to the new. As Grandmama Ema and she listened to the morning announcements and fanned themselves with funeral parlor paper fans, Max felt infinitely safe and totally at home sitting beside the aging warrior for Jesus. Ema Jones believed in keeping busy by doing God's work, which included educating and providing for the less fortunate. She was not one for judging others or idle gossip. When she wasn't working with her hands, she was praying for each of her twenty grandchildren.

Grandmama Ema died Max's thirteenth year. She probably prayed her way right up to Jesus.

FALLING IN THE OCEAN

The little girl in red sank to the bottom of the ocean. Blub, blub, blub. She had no body fat. She sank like a rock and watched the clear balls go up in the water. *Where do they come from?* Max thought. Blub, blub, blub. She couldn't swim. It wasn't like the mama and the daddy hadn't tried to teach the little girl in red. YMCA lessons didn't work either. My Boy dared her to walk on the edge of the boat while the grown-ups went below. "Come on. Give it a try. Come on. It isn't slippery." It was slippery. She could tell. My Boy was lying. But My Boy wanted her to try, so she tried. *Oops. Not very good at this*, thought Max. Into the ocean she went. Splash. Uncle Pete jumped in to get her off the ocean floor. He brought her back to the boat. The mama had worried eyes. My Boy had worried eyes. *What is wrong with their eyes? The ocean isn't so bad*, Max thought. *The little girl in red is O.K. It isn't the ocean that takes me away. I am always away. I always have been.*

GRANDMA MAXINE'S TINY TOWN

Grandma Maxine, the daddy's mama, was born and bred in a tiny town in Alabama, in the southern part of the state. She was the youngest of a large family. In Alabama, Max's grandmother was called Maxie Lou. The little girl in red's family would take Grandma Maxine with them when they visited Alabama. The three youngest children in Grandma Maxine's family were Maxie Lou herself, as the youngest, Uncle James Robert, the next youngest, and Aunt Bailey, the eldest of the three. Uncle James Robert and Grandma Maxine were called Irish twins because they were less than a year apart in age. Uncle James Robert and his wife, Aunt Gloria, still lived in the old rambling farm house where Maxie Lou grew up. Aunt Gloria made fried chicken for My Boy and mashed potatoes for Max, just like Maxie Lou had instructed. Aunt Gloria said the little girl in red had big brown eyes. My Boy and Max enjoyed swinging on the tire swing and climbing up the tree fort outside the old family home. Down the road, Aunt Bailey gave Maxie Lou's family a big bag of pecans, for the place had acres and acres of the nut. Cousin Billy was Aunt Bailey's son and lived around the corner from Aunt Baily. At Cousin Billy's house, the children swam in the big cement pool and jumped on the trampoline until their legs cramped.

The daddy had been raised in South Carolina, but he spent his summers in Alabama. He had many stories about the place. The all time favorite story that Grandma Maxine and the daddy would tell was about two of Maxie Lou's older brothers. They went to Florida to make money cutting down trees. They made enough cash to buy a new car. The brothers drove the car to the raging river, just south of Alabama. When the ferry was in the middle of the river, the car slipped off the ferry and fell beneath the rapids. There was no insurance in those days, so the brothers lost all they had worked for. They arrived home empty handed. Eventually the brothers returned to Florida and made money to buy another car. But the story of the sinking of the first car would be told over and over again.

THE TALL THIN GIRL

Puppies! The little girl in red saw the little dogs. It was the summer before third grade, and her family had moved into a rental house. While exploring her new territory, the little girl saw puppies over the back fence. She climbed the fence and ran to the puppies. She squatted on the ground and watched the mama dog love on her pups.

"Hey," a voice called out. "Hey you." The voice was coming from a woman standing next to a tall thin girl.

Max got up to run away.

"Don't run away" continued the woman. "It's okay."

The little girl in red froze, and the woman and her daughter walked over to her.

"What's your name?" asked the woman, in a kind voice.

"Max," the girl mumbled.

"Where do you live?"

The little girl in red pointed to her house.

"You're new around here. What grade are you going into?"

"Third."

"This is my daughter Caroline. She is going into third grade, too. I'll leave you two with the puppies."

It ended up that Caroline was in Max's homeroom that year.

The tall thin girl knew how to play games the little girl in red didn't know about. There was wiffleball, touch football, and basketball. Caroline was very good at these games, and though Max became more athletic the older she got, she never would catch up with her tall thin girl.

Caroline's backyard was next to the shopping center that held the drugstore with a soda fountain and the dime store with a frozen drink machine. Both had candy! Caroline and Max and the smart girl named Amy would walk to the shopping center almost every week day between third grade and seventh grade. They bought a lot of sugar over the years, between cherry Cokes and frozen drinks with cherry and cola mixed together, and candy. Oh, candy! There was never enough candy!

FIRST DAY OF THIRD GRADE

Brrriiinnggg

The bell hurt the ears of the little girl in red.

"Hello class! Welcome to third grade. My name is Mrs. Mayfield. I am your homeroom teacher. I will teach you spelling, grammar, art, and health. I will also take you to P.E., music, and lunch. Where you ended in math last year will determine what class you will go to in the middle of the day. Now everybody pull out your notebooks that we told your parents to get you."

Max began to panic. She did not have a notebook.

"Does everybody have their notebooks out?"

The panic grew in Max. The little girl in red put her head on her desk and started to cry. She wanted the mama to come pick her up and take her home.

Mrs. Mayfield walked up to Max, whose head was still on her desk. "What is wrong, Max?" Mrs. Mayfield already knew the little girl in red's name because the mama used to teach at this school.

Max kept her head down. She wanted the teacher to go away. She wanted the mama to rescue her.

"Max, do you have a notebook?"

"No," said a muffled voice between sobs.

"That's okay. I will call your mother tonight." Mrs. Mayfield walked away.

The little girl in red kept her head on the desk for a long time.

After lunch it was time to switch classes. Max had been put in the fast math class because math came fast in her head.

"Hello, children. My name is Mrs. Lee. I have been at this school longer than any other teacher. So I have taught a lot of children. I want to see how much you remember from last year, so I am passing out a sheet with some problems I want you to answer as quickly as possible."

Max looked all around her. She could not find her pencil. She realized she must have left it in the other classroom. The little girl in red squirmed helplessly in her desk.

"If you need a pencil, come get one. I have some extras," said Mrs. Lee in a kind voice.

Max grabbed a pencil. She walked back to her seat and answered the first problem on her sheet. The pencil point broke.

The little girl in red began to panic, just like she had earlier that day. She did not know where the pencil sharpener was. Max finally found the pencil sharpener with her frightened eyes. She dragged herself past the other children until she got to the loud grinding machine. The sharpener crunched at the pencil until it had a sharp tip once again. The little girl in red finally sat down and began to work on the math problems again.

When Max was about three-quarters through the problems, Mrs. Lee stood and said, "Okay class, turn in your sheet. Everybody should be finished."

But the little girl in red was not finished.

The other children turned in their sheets. The boy in front of Max said, loud enough for the entire class to hear, "Hey, turn it in! Didn't you hear the teacher?" The boy grabbed the paper from the little girl in red, and she dropped her head in defeat. Tears slid down her face once again. This was a really bad day.

Max knew the math. She had eaten up time getting a pencil and sharpening it. She was afraid the teacher would think she was stupid.

All of a sudden, Mrs. Lee was next to her. "Do you want a few more minutes to finish this?"

The little girl nodded her head, but she didn't look up. The teacher gave her back the paper, and Max finished the problems.

At home the mama asked about school.

"I don't want to go back."

"That bad, huh? How about you give it another day? Can you do that for me?"

The little girl nodded her head, but she didn't look up.

Of course, she had to go back to school. There was no other option.

CLEAN PLATE CLUB

On the second day of third grade, Mrs. Mayfield started something she called "The Clean Plate Club." All the way across the top of the chalk board there were paper plates with the children's names on them. Mrs. Mayfield explained that if you eat all of your lunch, your plate stays upright. But if you don't eat all of your lunch, your plate gets turned upside down and a check gets put on the back.

The little girl had never been a big eater. In fact, she was what people called a picky eater. Because of this, she had stayed thin. But she did not want her plate turned upside down. Mrs. Mayfield praised the children who finished all of their lunch. She scolded and asked why to the children who did not eat all of their food. Max did not want to be scolded and interrogated. She wanted to be praised and admired.

And so the little girl in red taught herself to choke down the food she did not like by drinking milk with it. And because there was little time to clean her plate, she learned to gobble her food instead of pick at it. After the first week of school, Max ate everything on her plate every single day of school. By the end of her third grade year, the little girl was no longer thin but average in weight. By the end of fourth grade, she had grown so much in height and weight that she was no longer one of the smallest in the class.

To this day, the Clean Plate Club brainwashing is difficult to resist, and Max has a difficult time controlling her eating habits.

RHINOCEROS

One week day before school, Max got tired of waiting on the mama to tell the children when to walk to school. So she made up a new game. She called it rhinoceros because she pretended she had a horn on her head. She ran across the room and threw herself head first into the big comfy chair. She found this great fun, and whatever she enjoyed, My Baby, who was three, wanted to try, too. So the little girl in red showed My Baby what she was doing, and My Baby gave it a try. Only, instead of landing in the big comfy chair's cushions, My Baby's forehead smashed into the front wood corner of the chair that holds the cushions to the big comfy chair. The wood corner split open My Baby's forehead, and the children screamed for the mama.

My Baby would need stitches, and whose idea was it anyway to play so rough? The little girl in red stood frozen. She didn't tell the mama she had thought up the game.

That evening at My Boy's football practice, My Baby was sitting barefoot in the mama's lap. While she was waving her foot through the grass, a piece of glass lodged itself in the top of My Baby's foot. She would need stitches twice in one day. The doctor looked at the mama kind of funny.

It was a crazy day, and nobody wanted to repeat it.

STRANGERS

There were some things that the little girl in red wished grown-ups would keep to themselves. The entire school was required to watch a film about strangers. In the film, two little girls hopped in a car of a man they did not know. Max and the rest of the third graders were removed before the film came to an end. My Boy saw the entire film. He told the little girl in red that the man ended up chasing the little girls in the woods. Max began to hide under her bed more than she usually did. She felt sure a stranger could not get her there. The mama demanded that the little girl in red go outside and play. She did not know why her daughter was acting odder than usual. My Boy finally told the mama about the film about strangers, and the mama tried to explain to her daughter that it was safe to play outside. But Max did not believe the mama. She could not get out of her head the picture of the little girls getting into the stranger's car. For months the little girl in red only left the house if her brother was with her. Finally, the family moved from that rental house and into the house they bought around the block. Max felt freer to go outside and play on her own, but her heart never forgot the lesson about the strangers.

MY BABY AND THE CAR

When My Baby was three and the little girl in red was in third grade, they jumped in the car with the mama. In those days there were no car seats for toddlers, and larger children and grown-ups rarely buckled up. My Baby and Max were in the back seat of the station wagon, and the mama was driving. As usual, the mama rolled to a stop at the local stop sign a few blocks from their house. Max's younger sister was experimenting with the lock on the door. As the mama started up again, My Baby opened the door on her side of the car. The force of the car picking up speed threw My Baby into the middle of the street. The little girl in red saw the entire incident, but the mama drove on. The mama did not see My Baby get thrown out of the car.

At first, no words came to the mouth of the little girl in red, just dry panic, as if she had cotton in her mouth. Finally she screamed, "MAMA!"

"Max, I don't have time for this. I am driving, and what have I said about not bothering me when I am driving?"

This was going to be harder than the little girl in red originally thought. Sometimes grown-ups just don't understand children.

"Mama! Lila!..."

"Lila what?"

"Lila fell out of the car!"

"WHAT?!!!!!!!!!" Screech, the car came to a quick halt.

Max saw the mama run as fast as she could to My Baby who was lying in the middle of the road. The mama snatched up My Baby. There was blood all over My Baby's face and the mama's shirt. Off to the doctor they went. My Baby's biggest injuries were the loss of one of her front baby teeth and a broken nose. The tooth was put back in its place until the permanent tooth came in. The nose is still crooked, even to this day.

FOOTBALL

One blustery afternoon in autumn, the mama barked at her two older boisterous children, "Go outside and play!"

Once outside, Max's brother called over his shoulder, "Come on. It's about time you learned to play ball." My Boy, who was called Peter by the grown-ups, had noticed that his sister did not make friends easily. He would begin her socialization training as only a fifth grade boy knew how. He would include her in the neighborhood football game. The little girl in red couldn't help but run after her brother because she adored him, and he made learning to play ball sound fun.

Together, the siblings trotted a block away to a neighbor's large flat front yard. When brother and sister arrived, some of the local boys were tossing a big brown egg back and forth. Only this egg was called a ball, and it didn't break.

When the medium sized boys went through their ritual of choosing up sides, My Boy stated, "My little sister comes with me. I'm going to show her how to play." There were no objections.

When the team opposite My Boy's had possession of the big brown egg, her brother whispered to Max, "I want you to knock over that kid in the blue shirt as soon as he catches the ball."

The little girl grimaced.

"Don't worry, it's okay," My Boy assured his sister. "You won't get into trouble. It's part of the game. Most likely they are going to throw the ball to that guy. So when I say 'Go,' I want you to take off running and then jump the boy, right after he makes the catch. You got that?"

The little girl smiled a crooked smile. That blustery autumn afternoon in 1969, Max's brother said, "Go!" And the little girl in red raced after the chosen child. In a flash, she had grabbed the receiver around the legs and pushed the astonished youth into the dirt. My Boy caught up with them. As he stood over the pair, he announced, "You can get off of him now Maxie. Let the poor boy up."

From that day forth, the little girl in red would wrap herself around the legs of the medium sized boys. My Boy's little sister earned the label of "The best tackler in the neighborhood."

Sometimes new boys would come to the neighborhood and proclaim they weren't playing with a girl who was just going to cry. But, Max didn't know to cry because the bumps and kicks from playing football didn't feel any different to her than any other touch to her sensitive skin. While she was hypersensitive to touch in a normal setting, the little girl was hypo-sensitive to the rough and tough play of the boys.

My Boy would remark to the new boy with a hint of pride in his voice, "You better shut up, or you'll be the one crying. Maxie is going to kick your butt."

The first time the little girl in red dragged a new boy to the ground, he would exclaim, "Damn, who is this girl? Where did she learn to do that?" And then the new boy would apologize to Max.

Now the parents of My Boy and the little girl in red didn't know anything about their daughter playing football with the boys. The mama would ask, "Max, you aren't playing ball with those boys are you?"

The little girl in red didn't have an answer. She didn't want to lie to the mama.

But her brother had no problem answering the question. "Oh no Mama. I don't let her play. She's been getting dirty by climbing trees while I play ball."

And so Max's football fame was only known by My Boy and the other medium sized boys because none of them wanted anybody to know a little girl could knock them down.

SITTING IN A TREE

Max sat at the top of a tree. No one knew she was there. She thought, *I am part monkey. I don't belong. Never will. I don't want to.*

The tree said, "I like the way you feel on me. Will you be my friend?"

The little girl in red thought, *Of course I will. I like you, tree. I like your leaves and bark, and you hide me.*

I'm going to build a spaceship next week. It will take me to the stars. They know my name. I'm going to sail away on a pirate ship. Mama wind will blow me to all the gold in the world. I'm going to live off of candy and coconuts. I'll have three baby chimpanzees and a giraffe. I'll swing from the trees. I am Supergirl and Batgirl, and I am part monkey, sitting at the top of the tree. No one knows I am here.

MY SHOES

The little girl in red had a pair of slip-on sneakers that she didn't have to tie. The mama said, "These shoes are old and dirty, and we need to throw them away."

"No." Max replied.

On Sunday, the family of the little girl in red went to a picnic in the park where the hippies hung out. Her parents were older than the hippies, but they were actors, and they liked the hippies. The mama had long beautiful hair that hung all the way to her bottom. The daddy had hair down to his shoulders. They looked like the hippies.

The daddy stopped and got a bucket of chicken. Max did not like fried chicken. She did not want to eat a bird. Birds were her friends. She ate potato salad instead. My Boy was eleven, and he liked chicken very much. My Baby was three, and she liked chicken very much. Max was eight. She was the only one who did not want chicken.

It was so hot that the children took off their shoes. They ran to the playground, and the grown-ups watched from far away. There was a slide with a tunnel on it. For a long time, the little girl in red disappeared from the grown-ups.

She thought, I am an army soldier fighting in a war. I parachute down the slide to save my country. I shimmy up one of the tall poles on the swing set. I am an explorer. I am the first girl to climb to the North Pole. I can see the whole world from up here.

The grown-ups said it was time to go.

Max's family climbed into the old station wagon. My Boy, My Baby, and the little girl in red climbed in the back seat. Max felt so free and happy from discovering the North Pole and from saving her country from enemies.

As they left the park, the little girl in red looked at her bare feet. "MY SHOES!" she shrieked. "MY SHOES, MY SHOES."

"Should we go back?" The daddy asked the mama.

"NO!" said the mama. 'We will not go back and get those horrible shoes. Max, it is time we get a new pair of shoes."

It was no use. They were from another planet. They did not understand. The little girl in red jumped to the "way back" of the station wagon and looked desperately out the back window. She could see the picnic table where her shoes were still waiting nicely where she had put them.

"Someone will steal my shoes," Max yelled to the people in the front of the car.

The mama replied, "Your shoes will be placed in the garbage where they belong."

The little girl in red couldn't see the picnic table anymore. She curled into a ball so far away from the grown-ups. No one can get me now.

She cried quietly, "My shoes, my shoes, my magic shoes." She thought, *How many times did I leap tall buildings with those shoes? I defended my country from the enemy in my shoes. How will I fight dragons and monsters and sharks without my magic shoes? How will I get to the North Pole next time? I was lucky today in my bare feet, but I do oh so much better in those slip on shoes. Oh, my shoes. The little girl in red needs her shoes. Rock the little girl in red. Keep her in a ball. Don't let them touch you. People hurt. Oh, God, I want my shoes. I need my shoes. They are mine. They are magic. Doesn't anybody understand? I want my shoes. Those shoes have killed millions of dragons, climbed millions of mountains, gone back in time to a million places. Those shoes have outrun polar bears and cobras and tigers. Those shoes are a part of me. Don't you see? That is me on that table in the park. That is me! That is me!*

GETTING ACCLIMATED

The little girl in red thought, *My mama must be from Mars, and my daddy is from Pluto. My sister is an Eskimo, and my brother is a spy. I hope I am right because I don't seem to fit in this earth skin. Sometimes I think there must be a planet or a country with people like me, people who aren't from this place. I don't seem to understand the language of the natives. Why don't I fit in? Why don't I belong? I wish I could fly away to my real home, but I am afraid of heights. And I wish I could burrow under the ground and go all the way to China, but I am afraid of small spaces. I wish I could tell the world who I really am, but I am afraid of earthlings. What if I never learn their weather, their customs, their crowds? Will I die alone in the skin that doesn't fit? I am so tired of this mission. When do I get to go to my real home? I watch Boo Radley in "To Kill a Mockingbird," and I know he knows how to get there. I watch Martin Luther king, and he talks of being free. Does anybody watch me?*

THE SMART GIRL

Amy was the smartest girl in third grade. Everyone knew it. One day, Amy approached Max and announced, "I like you! You're smart." From that day on, Amy was a friend of the little girl in red. Max loved to go to Amy's house. There were snacks, like milk with Hershey's chocolate syrup and cookies with fudge stripes on them. And there were card games and board games to play. Sometimes, they danced on Amy's father's feet. The little girl in red had never danced on her own father's feet. There was music to listen to and ping pong to play. And Amy joined Max and the tall thin girl, Caroline, on their daily journey to the drug store and dime store to get cherry cokes and frozen drinks and candy.

Without the tall thin girl and the smart girl, Max would have been very lonely. It wasn't that they were best friends, but more like neighborly sisters that kept an eye on one another. While the parents of the little girl in red were busy with jobs and extra-curricular activities Max depended on Caroline and Amy to watch out for her, and they did.

MEETING KERMIT

The daddy and his friends had become professional actors in North Carolina. They were told that Jim Henson and the Muppets would be coming. If the actors wanted to come an hour early to the show, Jim Henson, with Kermit the Frog, would come out front to meet the actors and their children. The daddy decided to take his children. But before they went, he explained to them that Kermit would look different than he does on the television. The daddy said that Kermit would be attached to Jim Henson, that Jim would have his hand in Kermit. The children didn't really listen to the daddy. They figured grown-ups didn't have a clue about things that pertain to children.

There was a medium sized crowd waiting for Kermit in front of the Puppetry Arts front steps. The little girl in red got pushed to the front of the crowd somehow, so that when Kermit and Jim appeared they came right up to her.

"Well, hello," said Kermit and Jim together. "How are you?"

Max was terrified. Jim Henson had his hand up the back end of Kermit the Frog. They didn't look anything like they did on T.V. The little girl in red just looked back and did not answer the frog, who had a man talking for him.

"Well," said Kermit and Jim, "I guess you aren't going to talk to us. I guess we need to find somebody else." And they moved on to another child who was willing to talk.

Max turned around and found her father in the back of the crowd. She did not feel safe at the front anymore. The little girl in red never saw Kermit the Frog the same again after that. She would always remember that somebody was talking for him. She would always remember that she felt safer with the daddy than with a stranger with a frog on his arm.

ACTING

Max's elementary school put on a play each year. Mrs. Mayfield was supposed to choose somebody from her class to be in the school play. She decided to have her class put on puppet shows. The children had to make the puppets and write their own scripts. The little girl in red and her partner were some of the last people to perform. Mrs. Mayfield kept telling the children before them to speak up. So when Max got behind the cardboard puppet theater, she yelled out her lines. She did not know that this would win her a spot in the school play, but it did. She was awarded a small part of Little Red Riding Hood in the school wide production of *Babes in Toyland*. She had to learn a short dance which was difficult for her, but she had no problem blurting out the two lines assigned to her. The little girl in red liked rehearsals, but she didn't particularly like the large crowd at the performance.

Around the same time, her parents decided to put Max in acting lessons. The acting lessons ended with a performance of *Hansel and Gretel*. There was no script. The children were left to their own devices, which made the little girl in red feel queasy in her stomach. Max was given the part of Hansel because she had short hair and looked a bit like a little boy. Gretel and the father were played by large sisters who did most of the talking in the play. The fact that they hammed it up took pressure off of the little girl in red. Max hung in there and even made it through the final performance in front of family and friends.

Because the daddy was doing his own professional acting, he had acting friends. Some of his friends called and asked if one of his children could be in an adult play with them. The little girl in red was standing next to the phone, and the daddy asked if she wanted to be in a play. She said sure, and there began an adventure of being in a play with adults. The play was about Santa Claus and Satan trading places and nobody being able to tell the difference until a little child is called upon. Each day, Max was picked up by a man and woman in a VW Bug. She was stuffed in the back with all their other gear. Her favorite person at the rehearsals was a man named Ramen. Ramen's part was Santa Claus who had switched with Satan. By the night of the performance, they had rehearsed so much that the little girl in red's part came naturally, and she was said to be a rather good little actor.

DECODING THE LANGUAGE

One spring, My Boy concluded that Max needed to smile and laugh more at the right times. The little girl in red laughed, but not so much when everybody else was laughing. My Boy pulled out one of the daddy's comedy albums, and he ordered his sister to sit on the plaid sofa. He played the album over and over every afternoon for a week. In the monologue about Moses's and the ten commandments, he explained that at church and in the Bible, Moses was an extra good person, but in the comedian's story, Moses acted like a normal person to God's extraordinary requests. This was funny because the comedian made Moses react the way we feel, not how we are supposed to act. So when Moses said, "Sure thing!" he is showing that he is doubtful about what God is asking him to do. Max listened intently to My Boy. She didn't understand everything her brother said, but she began to understand that funny stories were acceptable. My Boy continued to explain each line of each monologue and told the little girl in red why the words were funny.

Max did not learn to laugh at the comedian's jokes that year. That would come later. But she did learn to mimic the comic's style of speaking, with wit and in storytelling monologues. It was a similar style both the mama's and daddy's families used to pass on information as southern story tellers. But her brother slowed it down and broke it apart. My Boy had given the little girl in red a structure in which to decode the human language. Though she could understand a lot of what was said to her between the ages of three and eight, she had never understood how to respond with a lot of words. Not only had Max's brother opened a door so that her soul could communicate a little more with the rest of the world, he had given her a way to make more friends. Her gift for witty comebacks was considered a valuable asset by her future friends, even if she didn't see herself as being very funny. She saw herself as barely one step in front of the monsters that visited her most nights.

SHE'S HIDING UNDER THE TABLE: ONE WOMAN'S LIFE WITH ASPERGER'S AND DEPRESSION

PART TWO – THE MEDIUM GIRL IN MAROON

MEDIUM GIRL IN MAROON

Just before spring of her third grade year, Caroline, the tall thin girl, announced there was something called softball tryouts. She made it sound like so much fun that the little girl in red ran to her parents and begged to go.

The daddy took her on a Saturday morning to the softball tryouts. A man was throwing the ball to another man, and Max was told to try to hit the ball with a stick called a bat. After swinging the stick, the little girl in red was sent to the field with her new glove the daddy had bought at K-Mart. Max didn't know how to catch the ball yet, so she just stood in the way of the ball and let it hit her. Then she picked it up and threw it to the man who threw the ball to the next person with the stick. Apparently stopping the ball with her body made her a pretty good ball player, and she became a shortstop for the next four years. Max also became accustomed to bruises all over her body. Eventually, she would catch the ball more in her glove than with her body, but she would always revert to her original way of stopping the ball when she couldn't catch it.

Max's first team was called the Appaloosas. The Appaloosas would be wearing maroon uniforms. The little girl in red had never heard of the words appaloosa and maroon before that day. She had no idea what maroon would look like. But she felt excitement in her tummy, nonetheless.

When her uniform arrived, Max put it on and didn't want to take it off. She had become the medium girl in maroon.

THE SMART BABY

Third grade meant cursive handwriting and multiplication tables. My Baby was five years younger than Max. Whatever grade the medium girl in maroon was in was also the age of My Baby. When Max was in second grade, My Baby was two, and when the medium girl in maroon was in third grade, My Baby was three. So My Baby was three years old when Max was learning cursive handwriting and multiplication tables. One day, the mama asked where My Baby was, and the medium girl in maroon said, "Right here." The mama came in the room and saw Max practicing cursive handwriting. Right next to her, My Baby was also practicing cursive handwriting. And when the medium girl in maroon practiced her multiplication tables, My Baby practiced multiplication tables. Max hated being copied, but the mama said if My Baby could do multiplication and cursive writing then let her do it. The mama was a teacher, and she knew about these things. And so My Baby learned to write in cursive before she could print, and she learned her multiplication tables before she learned to add. She was a very smart baby.

GRANDMA MAXINE

Grandma Maxine grew up in Alabama, but as an adult her house was in South Carolina. The medium girl in maroon's grandmother was very tall and could touch her toes when she bent over. Grandma Maxine had a lot of framed pictures of her three grandchildren in her parlor. The grandmother took Max, My Boy, and My Baby to the dime store in town to pick out toys. Instead of cooking for them, she took her grandchildren, the daddy, and the mama to a restaurant. Everybody at the restaurant knew Grandma Maxine.

Grandma Maxine came to live with her only son and his family sometimes. She brought presents for everyone. The grandmother liked to watch her stories on the T.V. Dilly, the cat, loved to sit on her and purr. Grandma Maxine smoked cigarettes. She said she didn't inhale. The cigarettes gave her a special smell that the medium girl in maroon thought belonged only to her grandmother. Grandma Maxine liked My Boy the best. This hurt Max's heart. When the children fought, the grandmother always took My Boy's side. This made the medium girl in maroon cry. Grandma Maxine cheered up everybody by playing the piano without sheet music. Max calmed down. On Sundays, the grandmother made mashed potatoes for Max. It made the medium girl in maroon glad to have a grandma live with her.

DIRTY JOKES

Amy, the smart girl, and Caroline, the tall thin girl, would watch over the medium girl in maroon. But some of her time was still spent tagging along behind her brother, My Boy. This meant Max was hanging around fifth grade boys when she was still in third grade. The fifth grade boys were into telling dirty jokes. They would laugh and laugh, but the medium-sized girl felt bad after she heard each joke. She couldn't get the jokes out of her head. Round and round they swirled. She knew better than to tell the mama or the daddy about the jokes. My Boy said they would get mad. They just wouldn't understand a fifth grade boy custom. The facts of life, according to the older boys, were to be whispered and laughed at. Because of this Max no longer saw her brother as wise. Something was just not quite right. By the time the medium girl was in fifth grade and boys her age tried to shock her with the same dirty jokes she already had heard, she knew for sure that fifth grade boys weren't so smart.

JESUS AND ME

The medium girl in maroon thought, *We are best friends – Jesus and me. The preacher says that Jesus lives in my heart. I wonder if that means Jesus is a girl. Or maybe it just means a boy lives in my heart. I guess it really doesn't matter. What matters is that I get to carry Jesus around with me wherever I go. I am used to it because the preacher talks about Jesus being everywhere and knowing everything. Jesus talks to me because he is my special friend. He tells me that he loves me and that he is proud of me. Sometimes when I hide under the bed and no human can see me, I know that Jesus can see me. Jesus is better than magic because he can do miracles. I talk to Jesus, and I feel warm in my heart. The preacher says the good feeling in my heart is the Holy Spirit sent by Jesus.*

I can't talk to my daddy about Jesus. He doesn't believe in Jesus. I guess Daddy doesn't know that Jesus is portable and travels around with you and that Jesus is everywhere in the whole universe.

The mama at my house knows Jesus. She can't explain him all the time, but she knows him. She knows about the warm feelings. The mama takes my brother, sister, and me to church every time the doors are open and even when they are not because she is the church librarian. We work in her library, even when other people aren't in the church building. We go to choir, Sunday School, Wednesday night Bible study and Bible school in the summer. I like being in Jesus' house. He lives there when we come to see him on Sundays and Wednesdays. I never get tired of Jesus. In Sunday School and Bible study we hear stories of Jesus' antics while he was in human form. He stirred up a lot of trouble. I hope I have the courage to stir up trouble when I grow up.

PRESIDENTIAL PHYSICAL FITNESS TEST

Starting in fourth grade, the school children were tested on their physical abilities. It was called the Presidential Physical Fitness Test, and if you passed twice in one year, you got a patch. The medium girl in maroon loved the tests. There was a long jump, a sprint, and a long endurance run. But best of all for the girls was something called the flexed arm hang, where the girls held their heads above a metal bar for as long as possible. The boys had to do pull-ups, but the girls just had to hang. Since Max was still somewhat small for her age, she was able to hold her weight in the air for a very long time. It amazed the teachers and the other children. The medium girl in maroon loved the praise. She also loved the patch she earned each year. She was sure the President of the United States was proud.

PIANO LESSONS AND GIRL SCOUTS

The mama bought a new piano and put My Boy and the medium girl in maroon in lessons. At first the lessons were easy, and the teacher was a kind and patient woman. But as soon as Max was supposed to use both hands, she began to lag behind. My Boy quit in his second year of lessons. He simply refused to practice, but the medium girl in maroon wanted to please the mama. Instead, she sat in tears on the piano bench of her teacher. She just couldn't get one hand to cooperate with the other. This went on for four years, fourth to seventh grades, before the teacher told the mama it was no use. The mama was broken hearted. She had wanted at least one of her children to play like she did.

During the same time Max was in junior choir, softball, and Girl Scouts. My Boy was in Boy Scouts, and they went camping every month, no matter the weather. They were tough. But the medium girl in maroon's Girl Scout troop was not so tough. They barely camped out. Once they camped out in the leader's backyard, and another time they slept on the floor of a big lodge in the woods. Max was disappointed with the camping end of Girl Scouts. But there were other merits. She enjoyed getting badges. In particular, the entire troop took bowling lessons and earned their own special bowling badge. The medium girl in maroon liked learning a skill that could help her later on in life. All in all, piano lessons and Girl Scouts just didn't add up to the thrill of softball and the pride she felt when she wore her maroon uniform.

JASON

Cousin Jason had four names, something that the medium girl in maroon had not known was possible before he told her that fact. Jason Roger Jones Lawson! He was the fourth of Aunt June's six children, and, though three years Max's senior, he let her tag along sometimes. The medium girl in maroon was mesmerized by her cousin's wide variety of feats. Jason could grow beautiful flowers out of the dirt. He used a patch of land on the side of the rambling clapboard house and tried his hand at anything that would spring forth from the South Carolina gray sand.

Jason also collected matchbook covers from exotic places. He showed Max his rainbow of match covers and told her how far they had come. She knew that she could never write to strangers and ask for something that had not already been offered. It had never occurred to the medium girl in maroon that things such as matches were to be collected. She collected rocks because they sang to her. But Jason didn't collect rocks. He and his two brothers had a gigantic collection of comic books. My Boy had one of these too. But Jason and his brothers had outdone themselves. Their stack went on and on. Max's cousin knew facts about wars and battles, important moments in America's history. He lined up his tiny plastic soldiers all over the front yard and reenacted times gone by.

Jason was kind to the twenty something cats that roamed the family farm. When kittens were born, he prepared a clean, warm box for them. Jason told the medium girl in maroon not to squeeze the kittens and make them squeal. Sometimes the kittens got very sick and died. Max watched her cousin bury them in the kitty cat cemetery in the backyard.

The medium girl in maroon's favorite place to visit Jason was on the front porch in the rocking chairs, after the sun went down and a cool breeze tickled their skin. They slapped at an occasional mosquito. Her cousin told her about living in a small town in South Carolina and asked questions about what it was like for Max to grow up in the suburbs of North Carolina. Because there was no hurry, and because the medium girl in maroon didn't have to look into Jason's eyes, and because he treated her like a peer, she learned to say more than she ever had before. It was Jason who made Max feel the most welcome she had ever felt since she came to live on this planet.

There would be others, but Jason was the first. He was one of the keys to helping the medium girl in maroon grow up in a society with humans. Each summer of her youth, she rocked and talked with her cousin on that rambling, front porch. Sometimes she can still hear the soft murmur of their voices on a cool summer's night.

DEAD IS...

Granddaddy no longer took the medium girl in maroon and Penny to the back bedroom and creaked open the antique dresser drawer that hid the chewy orange slice candies from Grandmama's sharp eyes. The cousins got hot dust in their throats, and their legs cried out from walking so far to the graveyard to see the place where they have laid his bones. The screen porch rocker no longer sings to the beat of the Bobwhites. Max's family ride and ride in the sticky, hot station wagon to a place now called "Grandmama's." Granddaddy no longer licked the whisper thin paper to roll his cigarettes, and he didn't wear his starched white shirts with little burn holes.

I don't know where Granddaddy went, thought the medium girl in maroon. *I see his shiny blue eyes in the framed pictures in Grandmama's "hush-hush" parlor. In the pictures, Granddaddy and I have the same crooked smile. I miss you Granddaddy. When are you coming home?*

Love,
Your Rocking Buddy
Maxie Taxie

BLOODY STORIES

It was a blistering hot day in the summer after fourth grade. Caroline, also known as, the tall thin girl, and Max didn't care. They walked in the heat to the store anyway. Caroline got a cherry coke at the drug store. The medium girl in maroon got a cherry frozen drink at the dime store. When Max went to pay for her drink, the teenage girl at the counter asked how she was doing. Instead of saying the usual, "Fine," the medium girl in maroon piped up with "My little sister just got stitches. She is only four."

The teenager, who was quite bored with her job queried, "Oh yeah, has she had any other stitches?"

"She sure has!" Max was delighted at her chance to talk. She spoke so rarely and now she had an audience for some of her first storytelling.

Caroline, who was looking rather pale, mumbled, "Let's go."

"In a minute," the medium girl in maroon said impatiently, for she was excited. This was her sister's fourth set of stitches, which meant there was plenty to say.

"I'm going out," the tall thin girl mentioned, as she pushed the glass door into the hot air.

Max stayed and told all her stories. It was very gratifying. The dime store clerk had been a great audience. When the medium girl in maroon walked outside, Caroline was lying on the ground face down. She liked to pull practical jokes and had, in fact, played this very joke before.

"Oh, get up," said Max. "I'm on to you."

The tall thin girl raised her head and blood trickled from her chin.

"Oh," was all the medium girl in maroon could think to say.

The teenage clerk came outside and saw what was happening. "Where are her parents?"

"At home."

"Go get them."

Max took off running. She could feel the hot wind in her lungs. The distance to Caroline's house seemed a lot longer than usual. When she finally made it, she knocked on the door, out of breath. Caroline's brother, Stuart, came to the door. "What's wrong? Where's Caroline? I thought you two went to the store."

"She fell. There's blood."

"Dad!" yelled Stuart. "Caroline is hurt."

It never occurred to the medium girl in maroon to ask for a ride. She ran the distance back to the store.

The tall thin girl's father was putting Caroline in the car. They were going to the emergency room.

Later that day, Caroline came over to Max's house. She didn't have stitches. She wouldn't let the doctor sew up her chin. Instead, she had bandage strips trying to keep the wound closed. Because of this, the tall thin girl would end up with a larger scar than if she had had stitches.

When Caroline went to college in south Alabama, everybody new to her asked about her scar. She told them about the hot day and Max's bloody stories. "You're famous," she said to Max some time later.

"Hmm," was all the Max could think to say.

THE HUTTMANS

One of the great adventures of Max's life was visits to the Huttmans. Mr. Huttman and the daddy worked together as computer programmers in Raleigh, NC and once again worked together in Charlotte, NC. The Huttmans' lived one school district away from the medium girl in maroon's family. Max had a brother three years older than she and a sister five years younger than she. But the Huttmans' family unit was quite different. They had five children between Max and her little sister's age. There was Martha, Dorothy, Justin, Carl, and Kindel. From the medium girl in maroon's point of view, all those children so close in age meant more fun than she had at her house. A typical weekend happened like this: Max's family would be visiting the Huttmans on a Friday evening. Martha and Dorothy Huttman would approach their mother and father and say, "Can Max spend the night?" They didn't ask the medium girl in maroon this question. The assumption was that she wanted to spend the night, and she did. Both sets of parents would consent, and that is how Max got drafted into the Huttman household for 24 hours.

There were bikes to ride and tag to play, woods to explore and a football to run. There was an off limits cliff to peek over and not tell the parents what they were doing. There were board games to argue over and food to be gobbled. It was an adventure Max will never forget. She was thankful that parents have friends so that their daughter got pulled into a family that knew how to play.

THE HALL

The medium girl in maroon tried very hard to be a good girl. She did not like to get into trouble at all. She listened and obeyed her parents and teachers as much as possible. It was not a surprise that she had gotten to fifth grade without going into the dreaded hall. The hall was where bad boys and girls were sent when they got into trouble in the classroom. It was one step away from the principal's office. Max's brother, My Boy, knew the hall quite well. He had a problem with talking when he wasn't supposed to, but that was not a problem for the medium girl in maroon. Getting her to talk was more of a problem than getting her to be quiet.

One long day in fifth grade, the boy in front of Max turned around and started talking to her at length. The medium girl in maroon could not hear the teacher, and she finally told the boy to be quiet. The teacher did not see or hear the boy. She only heard Max.

The teacher looked at the medium girl in maroon and pointed to the hall. "Max, go to the hall for talking."

Max was shocked. She had never been to the hall before, and she didn't deserve to go to the hall for this incident. But she didn't argue. Arguing with a teacher meant going to the principal's office.

The medium girl in maroon dropped her head and dragged her feet into the hall. She leaned against the wall while big tears dropped from her face.

Then the unimaginable happened. The principal came down the hall and asked, "What are you doing in the hall?"

Max just cried.

The teacher came out of the classroom and said, "Don't talk when I am talking ever again."

The medium girl in maroon shook her head in agreement and tried to wipe the tears away. She was still crying when she took her seat again. She knew she would never forget going into the hall. She would never go there again.

THE LAWSONS

The medium girl in maroon continued to go to Aunt June's every summer. On Saturdays, Aunt June's husband, Uncle Lawrence, loaded up the Volkswagen van with kids for a trip to Pineville. June and Lawrence Lawson lived in a tiny town in South Carolina. They went grocery shopping in Pineville because it was cheaper than the local shops and had a wider variety of food. Before he went shopping, Uncle Lawrence dropped all the children at the library. The library was a wonderful place to explore. Penny and Max would turn in books they had already read and checked out as many books as they were allowed. The cousins would leave their books at the library to take a walk around town. First, they skipped to the newsstand to skim through the magazines they had no intention of buying. Next, the girls went to the bakery to get donuts and cookies. Last, they got fountain drinks at the drug store. By the time Penny and the medium girl in maroon got back to the library, it was only a short wait for Uncle Lawrence to pick up everybody.

During the weekdays when the girls weren't running around the pool or reading, they played Spades with the big kids. Spades is card game with partners. The object is to take the most tricks. Max was good at taking tricks. To increase their chances at winning she paid attention to what her partner played. It felt good in the medium girl in maroon's heart to win and to be appreciated for her card skills.

Penny and Max decided to collect as many glass soda bottles as they could find for money to spend at groceries. Without asking permission, they walked down the highway away from town, towards the dump. They each gathered a brown paper sack full of bottles. Unfortunately, they hadn't thought through the adventure. The girls picked up bottles all the way to the dump. They should have left them on the ground and then picked them up on the way to town. Instead, they had full bags at the dump and had to walk all the way back to town with them. Penny and the medium girl in maroon had to put down the heavy sacks multiple times to rest. It was slow going, but they eventually made it to the store. They were able to buy all the penny candy they had ever imagined getting in one day. The cousins also got prized ice cream cones and drinks in glass bottles to take home for later. When Aunt June saw her daughter and niece with so much candy, she asked where they had gotten all the money. When the girls explained, Aunt June yelled, "You did what?" But she let Penny and Max keep all their candy.

Treasure Hunts and Homespun Plays

When the cousins got together at Grandmama's house, their combined creative energies became genius. They all read a book about children on a treasure hunt, and so they made treasure hunts for each other with clues that sent them running all over the farmhouse and the surrounding property. It was like fresh air turned on high. At the end there was always a tiny prize for each of the hunters, and it made it all the more fun.

Amanda was the one who started the script for the first play. She thought it would be funny to make Max, the smallest of the actors, Frankenstein's monster. She soon dropped her writing, but T.J. picked it up. Although he did not find it humorous that the monster was so short, he decided to stick with the parts. The monster was ravaging the village, and the problem needed to be solved. The medium girl in maroon loved her part. She got to wear cold cream with green dye and growl at everybody.

The audience was indeed surprised by the effort of their offspring. Grandmama looked reflective. No telling what she was thinking about the generation of grandchildren before her. The next morning the green dye would not leave Max's face, and so she went to church as she was. Again Grandmama did not say a thing.

The next year, T.J. decided on a comedy. The Jolly Green Giant, played by Cousin Jeremy, could not find his Little Green Sprout, played by the medium girl in maroon's baby sister, Lila. An inspector was called in to find the Sprout, and, of course, she was under the giant's foot the entire show. Max was a frog. She didn't know why she was frog. She just was. And she got to wear a green sewn mask. Because her part was of little importance to the plot, the medium girl in maroon became quite bored in rehearsals, that is, until little Cousin Walt, Aunt Lydia's son, threw open the doors releasing the hound named Percival. "Go, dog, go!"

Walt screamed at the dog. Max chuckled and T.J. was perturbed that his production was delayed. The "Go, dog, go" scene played itself over many times, and finally Max was happy to be assigned to watch Walt.

During the production itself the medium girl in maroon was hot and bothered by her giant mask, but she couldn't help smile when Walt jumped up and said, "That's Macksie!"

T.J. also wrote a commercial in which the entire crew sang, "Casey's Coffins are so fine…When it's time for you to go, Casey's is the place to know." Then out popped Max's little sister from a trunk that was a pretend coffin. The audience was indeed shocked. But they clapped and asked for more. Everybody had found a way to have some fun that hot summer evening, and Grandmama took it all in with her watchful eye.

A Real Life Nightmare

It was one of the first evenings of the summer. School was out, and fun was around the corner. The medium girl in maroon had finished fifth grade. She ran up the hill to the smart girl Amy's house and found almost the entire neighborhood playing kickball or watching the game. Amy, who was watching, said to Max, "I have somebody for you to meet. I think you will like her. You both do a lot of living in your imaginations. Her name is Sally."

They walked over to where Sally was standing.

Amy spoke first. "Sally, this is Max. You two remind me of each other. You should become friends."

Amy walked away and left the medium girl in maroon with the girl she did not know. For a moment, Max didn't know what to expect.

Sally's eyes shone as she smiled. She acted like she had always known the medium girl in maroon. "Let's play."

"I want to be a pirate." It wasn't' something Max usually admitted. She was too old to be pretending.

But Sally didn't even hesitate. "Where's the buried treasure?"

The medium girl in maroon smiled a crooked smile, "My pet monkey will show us the way."

And so the like-minded played pirates until Sally's mother called her in. It was a great way to start summer vacation.

"Meet you tomorrow?" asked Sally.

"I'm going to my aunt's in South Carolina. But I will come see you when I get back."

The medium girl spent her usual three weeks at Aunt June's. She had a grand old time. Penny even came back to NC with her to visit. When she got home, Max ran to Amy's to ask where Sally lived. She was ready to get going with this incredible new friendship. There were so few people who understood her.

Amy hesitated and finally said, "I have to tell you something about Sally. She died."

The medium girl in maroon just stared at Amy.

Amy continued, "It was a horrible accident, the worst kind. You see, my next door neighbor has a small plane, and he was working on it in his driveway. A group of the neighborhood kids were enjoying the breeze of the propeller. Sally was one of those kids. I was here in my room when I heard the screams. My parents ran out to see what had happened and told me to stay in the house. It seems that Sally's mother and little sister were driving by, and Sally ran toward her mother's car. She forgot about the airplane's propeller and ran through it. Parts of her body were thrown everywhere. It took a while to find most of her. Anyway she's dead. The funeral was a few days ago."

Max just kept staring. She couldn't think of a thing to say. She was horrified. God had given her a new friend that was so much like herself, and now God took her away in the most awful way. She felt immense pain.

Amy interjected into the medium girl's thoughts. "My mother wants us to go down to Sally's house and visit with her mother and sister. Will you go with me?"

That's just what they did. They went to Sally's house, only Sally wasn't there, and her sister now had two of everything. There was a big tank of colorful fish in the living room. Sally's mother thanked the girls for coming.

Max never told her parents about that day. She withdrew and became even quieter with her parents, except for when she was having nightmares in which she tried to save Sally from the propeller. She screamed out and knew more than ever that monsters live in the dark. She felt even greater loneliness than she had known before.

To this day Max doesn't like to walk in front of the driveway where Sally was killed. She is still spooked and scared she will find a part of

Sally's body. It is a horrible nightmare that never should have happened to a medium sized girl.

THE CRUCIBLE

"Take Max with you," the mama yelled from her bubble bath.

"What?" the daddy yelled back.

"I said, take Max. She is our middle child, and she seems to be in the middle of every fight. Take her with you and I'll have peace tonight."

"Get your coat, Maxie," the daddy said. "Hurry up. I can't be late."

In the old, pine green Volvo, the daddy recited his lines. The medium girl in maroon had to be quiet. She looked out the window at the passing cars, their lights blinding her eyes.

There was no audience in the theater, just the actors, director, and crew needed to produce a community play.

The daddy said to his daughter, "You be good. Sit here and watch the play." He left her in the padded seat where she usually fell asleep.

That night the actors called for their lines a little less than before, and the director didn't interrupt with suggestions as much. The production was shaping up into a play, in particular *The Crucible*. The play was about a real life witch hunt that took place in the northeastern United States. By watching the play, Max felt she was learning about the world of grown-ups. In the world of grown-ups, paranoia ran amuck, and finger pointing led to death.

The medium girl in maroon was pretty sure she would stay a kid a little longer.

MY BOY'S T.V.

My Boy owned the T.V., or at least he thought he did. The daddy and the mama were very busy people with working, acting, and local politics. That left My Boy, Max, and the television alone for many hours together. My Baby was at the new babysitter's house. Since Max's older brother thought he owned the T.V., he taped a list of what he was going to watch to the side of it. If the medium girl in maroon attempted to change the channel, she was clobbered by her brother. So Max did not watch as much television as My Boy. She did not like most of his shows.

There were two shows My Boy did let her watch for some unknown reason, *The Waltons* on Thursday night and *The Partridge Family* on Friday night. The medium girl in maroon loved these shows. She loved to pretend she was in a large family that loved to be together, instead of out taking care of the world. But then the shows would be over, and the reality was that My Boy owned the T.V.

THROWING THE BALL

My Boy's favorite pastime was watching the television, but he grew tired of his shows once in a while. That is when My Boy suggested the medium girl in maroon and he play catch in the street below their house. Playing catch meant that sometimes Max's brother threw the softball hard and fast, and it burned into the girl's glove. Sometimes, he threw it high like a pop fly. But a lot of the time the ball just went wherever it felt like going. It went over Maxie's head, hit her shins, or bounced into her face. It wasn't that the medium girl was any better at throwing the ball than her brother. But it did mean that she became a better fielder because she had to learn to catch just about anything, if she didn't want to spend her time chasing down the ball. Without trying, My Boy had made his sister a great ball player by his throwing wild pitches. Days and weeks and months and, finally, years of throwing the ball back and forth made Max a valuable fielder. Although she quit her softball team after her seventh grade year, she would pick softball back up in eleventh grade, and she would find out then that her fielding skills were superior to those of most other girls her age. She could owe it to her brother getting bored with television and asking his sister to play catch and to the fact that he never really improved in his ability to throw the ball in a straight line.

THE SIXTH GRADE PLAY

Every year, the sixth graders of the Elementary School put on an original play that they wrote themselves. Three boys and four girls were chosen to write the play the year Max and Amy were a part of the writing team. The medium girl in maroon had been in an adult play and also watched her father and mother act. She had a good idea for the play. How about if Charlie Brown from the *Peanuts* comic strip got hit in the head with a baseball and became an excellent but arrogant ball player, instead of his usual humble, bumbling self? Eventually, the rest of the Peanut gang would get fed up with the new, improved Charlie Brown, and so they would hit him in the head with the ball again, so that they could get back the old, lovable Charlie Brown. The rest of the writing team loved the idea and went behind the stage curtain to flirt. They left Max to write the rough draft of the script. When the other sixth graders disappeared to most likely practice kissing, the medium girl in maroon felt weird inside her heart. She had no desire to kiss anyone and didn't understand the urge of the other children her age. This made her feel quite lonely and left out, but she didn't see a way to change the fact that she didn't want to be kissed.

The teachers loved the rough draft. The main change was that there needed to be as many parts as possible for as many six graders to be in the play. Max had *Peanuts* books at home and was able to scan the pages to get as many characters for the play that she could find.

After being the main writer of the play the medium girl in maroon expected a big part in her own play. Instead, she was given one line, and she was sorely disappointed. Then she was surprised to find out that her mother had been invited to direct the play. Again, this made no sense to her heart. It was her play. Max was the authority on how it was to be acted, and she should be Charlie Brown, too. After all, the play was really about her humble bumbling self and the fact that no one would like her if she really shined. But she would never know for sure if she would shine. The teachers didn't know the other writers had been flirting and left the script to the medium girl in maroon. A popular boy would be playing Charlie Brown, and her own mother would usurp her as the director. It was difficult growing up different from the other children. Somehow, Max knew Charlie Brown would understand.

MISCHIEF

The medium girl in maroon often found herself in spots she wished she didn't have to live through, but she did live through them nonetheless.

There was the time Roy challenged her to a fist fight. Max had never participated in a fist fight. She was used to wrestling when she fought her brother. But Roy didn't wrestle. He repeatedly punched the medium girl in maroon in the face. She was about to cry, when Grandma Maxine called her into the house. She was never so happy to have a meddling grandmother than that day.

Another time Caroline, also known as the tall thin girl, Roy, and the medium girl in maroon were playing Truth or Dare. Caroline dared Max to kiss Roy on the lips. And so her first kiss was a miserable affair that she wished she could forget.

The last piece of mischief on which the medium girl in maroon wished she could turn back the time tables was the day she and Caroline tried smoking. The cigarettes had a nasty taste, but Max didn't have the guts to say no. So there she was smoking, something she said she would never do. She was more than happy to give it up as quickly as she had started.

All three times the medium girl in maroon wished she had said no, but she didn't say anything. She just did what she was asked to do.

THE POSTER CONTEST

Caroline, also known as the tall thin girl, had a great idea. How about Amy, also known as the smart girl, Max, and she enter the Fall Carnival poster contest? So they went to the dime store, got posters and markers, laid them out on the sidewalk, and began drawing. Max decided to draw one of the monsters that had plagued her ever since she had been a little girl. The fall carnival came just around Halloween. So she drew Gus in all his gore. It was rather cathartic, since she never talked about the monsters. Interestingly, Gus won the poster contest. The medium girl in maroon was called up to the office and handed the $5 prize. The principal said, "You've got a great imagination!" Only Max knew Gus was more than her imagination. He was very real to her.

The carnival itself was pure fun. The three girls ran down the hill to the school house and scared themselves in the spook house, threw softballs at the dunking machine, and walked in circles for a cake. They fished for prizes, threw sandbags into a big sturdy board with holes, and tossed hoops around poles. When they didn't win a cake on the walk they bought one of the homemade baked goods for the medium girl in maroon's birthday which was three days after Halloween.

Gus the monster had won Max $5 to spend at the carnival, instead of her having to ask her parents for money. This gave the medium girl in maroon a sense of pride. She was a bread winner.

SEVENTH GRADE PLAYS

With seventh grade came a drama club that cropped up for one year only. The outcome was a play called *Cinderella Revisited*. At the same time, the medium girl in maroon earned a bit part in the annual school-wide play. It was a disappointment, but she was rewarded by a large part with the drama club. In *Cinderella Revisited*, Cinderella is an obsessive compulsive house cleaner. Her stepmother and stepsisters want her to go to the ball to get her out of the house. Enter a bumbling, rag-tag Fairy Godmother who is assigned to trick Cinderella into going to the ball. Max got to be the Fairy Godmother. It fit her bumbling image. Although there were a lot of lines to memorize, the medium girl in maroon loved hamming it up in front of her peers on the day of the production. She even kicked a rain boot off the stage by accident, which only added to the part and also to Max's reputation for being funny without even trying. Max found it very satisfying being an actor, but she never acted again after that day. Adolescence was on its way, which made the medium girl in maroon a lot more shy.

GOING TO WASHINGTON

When she was asked at the end of her sixth grade year if she would be a patrol in her seventh grade year, Max answered quite honestly, "No." It was a shock for anybody to turn down the honor. But she didn't want to get up so early, that is, until seventh grade came. Both Amy and Caroline were patrols, and she was used to walking to school with them. So she volunteered in the school library. But that became boring because the medium girl in maroon had done so much library work already, since her mother was a church librarian. Eventually, Max was asked to be a substitute patrol because when the regular patrols got sick, they needed a replacement. Since there were about twenty patrols, the medium girl had to work almost every day. Whereas the regular patrols were assigned to one post, Max enjoyed her variety from substituting. She also enjoyed her few days off when no one called her to substitute.

At the end of the year, the patrols were rewarded with a week-long trip to Washington. There was an entire train with kids from the medium girl in maroon's part of North Carolina. It was like kid paradise. There were adult chaperones, but they monitored the train only randomly. The boys were separated from the girls by about three cars. This led to note swapping. When the adults came through the car, the girls gave them notes to be delivered to certain boys, and the adults delivered notes from the boys.

Max had no desire to send a note to a boy, but she was expected to join the fun. Because of peer pressure, she chose a boy who wasn't getting very many notes, John. So the medium girl sent two notes, but John didn't answer, so she was off the hook. Caroline, Max, and a new girl named Donna were roommates in Washington. They had many wonderful talks without the supervision of adults. Every part of Washington. was a new adventure. It was breathtaking for the medium girl in maroon. She had never known such a good long, time away from home that was not at her Aunt June's home. And the train trip back to NC was just as fun as the trip to D.C. Max was surprised she could have so much fun away from her family. But that is exactly what she did.

SHE'S HIDING UNDER THE TABLE: ONE WOMAN'S LIFE WITH ASPERGER'S AND DEPRESSION

PART THREE – THE GIRL IN BEIGE

GIRL IN BEIGE

"Come here," said Uncle Oscar. He led Max to his bedroom in the old farmhouse. Uncle Oscar pulled from his closet an old army shirt with the sleeves cut short. "Here. Take it. It's yours."

Max put the giant shirt over her t-shirt. She was now the girl in beige because she wore the shirt almost every day that summer before eighth grade.

One of the things that Max liked about the large army shirt was that it covered her blossoming body. During her high school years she did not want to show off her body. She preferred to hide it under large t-shirts, sweatshirts, and baggy pants. Other girls were wearing the latest fashion. Max, on the other hand, went to the local salvage store and bought two pairs of ragged fatigues that she wore almost every day in eleventh and twelfth grades.

The mama was horrified by Max's beige shirt and, later, the olive pants. Aunt Lydia said, "Just think. There is a lot less laundry."

THE DIVORCE

It was summer. That fall Max would start a new school. The eighth grade was attached to the high school, and so she would be riding the bus with her older brother as she started this new journey.

While she was watching Saturday morning cartoons with My Boy, the daddy asked the girl in beige to join him in the living room. This was unusual. The daddy never picked out Max to join him in the living room. This made the girl in beige feel queasy in her tummy. She left her brother watching the television and followed her father. My Boy watched from the corner of his eye. He had already been to the living room.

Standing at the far end of the large living room was the mama. She had a tear stained face. This was a shocking scene for Max. It had been a long time since her parents had stood together in the same room. The girl in beige felt outnumbered.

The daddy started the conversation. "Your mother and I are getting a divorce. She and Lila are moving to an apartment. Peter is staying here with me. It doesn't make sense to take him away from his friends and school. That leaves you. We have decided to let you pick who you want to live with."

Max stood in shock. She didn't say anything. It was too much at once. The mama was leaving with My Baby. My Boy was staying with the daddy. What?

"Who do you want to live with?" prompted the mama.

The question was unfair. The girl in beige wanted everybody in one place. But she had to admit she was tired of the mama and daddy fighting. She didn't want to leave her home, so the girl mumbled, "I'll stay with Daddy."

"What!" exclaimed the mama. "You can't choose your father!" The mama started to cry and crossed the room to Max. She tried to pull her daughter into her arms, but the girl in beige pulled free and curled up in a ball on the sofa.

"Leave me alone," wailed Max.

The daddy said nothing. But the mama followed the girl and pleaded with her.

The girl in beige didn't budge. She closed her eyes and pretended like the mama and daddy were gone. "Leave me alone," she pleaded.

Finally the mama and daddy really were gone and Max was alone, very alone.

UNCLE ABNER

After Max's parents announced their divorce, the mama took her three children on vacation to Aunt Lydia's house. The girl in beige lived with her father but she saw the mama on weekends and on vacation. Aunt Lydia's husband, Uncle Abner, had become a general and was second in command at an army base. Uncle Abner, or General Nolham, thought it would be fun for his nieces and nephew to see the base. He handed the children over to his personal assistant, the Lieutenant, and his chauffer, the Sergeant. The Lieutenant was a stiff, nervous young man who said little to the children. But the Sergeant was a likable, older man who was a veteran of the Vietnam War. He showed Max, My Boy, and My Baby his scars where he had steel kneecaps because he had been in an explosion when he was lying in his tent.

The first stop for the Lieutenant, Sergeant, the girl in beige, My Boy, and My Baby was the helicopter museum. It was a hanger with old helicopters in it. Max did not want to get close to the helicopter blades because she was reminded of Sally running through the airplane propeller. Nobody seemed to notice her reluctance.

The second place the Lieutenant told the Sergeant to drive was to the helicopter simulators. My Boy and the girl in beige thought it was fun to wreck their pretend helicopters. The Sergeant laughed along with them. But the Lieutenant saw no humor in the situation.

Next, the Lieutenant announced they were going to the air traffic control tower. The children climbed the steps that went up and up. They looked out over the horizon for miles. Seven-year-old My Baby announced they were to race back down the steps. My Baby won the race, with the Sergeant in a close second. My Boy and Max came in third and fourth. And the Lieutenant, who didn't seem to have his heart in it, came in last. My Baby shouted, "Slow poke, slow poke. You are a slow poke."

A group of young officers, who were fixing their parachutes, heard My Baby. When the Lieutenant walked by the officers, they all chanted, "Slow poke, slow poke. You are a slow poke." The Lieutenant flushed red. The Sergeant's eyes smiled.

It was time to pick up Uncle Abner. My Baby announced that she wanted to count garbage dumpsters because there were so many. So My Baby and the Sergeant began to count. When Uncle Abner joined them, he counted, too. The girl in beige's younger sister pointed out that the Lieutenant hadn't found any dumpsters. Uncle Abner, being the general, barked at his assistant, "Lieutenant! If my niece wants to count garbage dumpsters, then that is what we will do." The Lieutenant pointed to a dumpster. My Baby claimed she had already counted it.

The Lieutenant was also in trouble because the children had missed the fly-by for the helicopter graduation. He was not having a good day.

When the children returned to the house, Aunt Lydia said to Max, "You did not help the Lieutenant today. His wife called and told me how you gave him a hard time."

"It was Lila," the girl in beige whined.

"But you were in charge," corrected her aunt.

Max was left with a bad feeling in her stomach. She didn't like being in charge of her sister, but it was a part of being older, she supposed.

It was thought that the girl in beige could help with Walt. Thirteen years separated Walt, the youngest of his family, and his next sibling, Reide. Aunt Lydia got pregnant with Walt when she was forty. She could use all the help she could get. At age four, Walt liked to watch *Sesame*

Street as often as possible. He would rock back and forth and say, "I am the Count. Do you know why they call me the Count? Because I love to count. Ha ha ha."

One day Reide was supposed to drive Max, Lila and Walt to the officer's pool. Afterwards, they were supposed to pick apples at the home of a friend of Aunt Lydia's. Reide got to talking to the lifeguard and forgot about apples. Aunt Lydia drove to the pool and yelled at Reide, "I'm so mad I could spit." This was one of the funniest things the girl in beige and My Baby had ever heard. To this day they giggle when they picture their aunt screaming those words.

EIGHTH GRADE

Eighth grade meant riding the bus, instead of walking down the hill. It meant lockers with complicated combinations and hallways filled with students looking for classes. It meant six classes, plus homeroom. The girl in beige was overwhelmed and lost, without anything to hold onto. She made more "B"s than she had ever done before in her school career. She would recoup in ninth grade and stay on the A track from there on out. But in the meantime, eighth grade meant a girl in art class would accuse Max of having a crush on Caroline's brother. The girl in beige got so enraged that she threw the girl off her stool. That meant a "U" in conduct. Eighth grade meant required Physical Education was on the opposite corner of the giant school from the eighth grade hall. P.E. had one-piece stretchy suits that showed off your body. Eighth grade meant Caroline and Amy were in only one class each with Max, and she was in classes with a sea of strangers. It meant long lunch lines and trying to figure out where to sit. Eighth grade was one of the hardest transitions the girl in beige had ever known.

BASKETBALL

"I don't want to try out for basketball by myself. Will you try out with me?" Caroline asked the girl in beige. Caroline was tall and built like a basketball player. Max was short and stocky like a bulldog. Caroline had played basketball most of her life with her two ball-playing older brothers. The girl in beige had barely touched a basketball.

"Okay." It wasn't like there were many sports open to girls in that day. When she grew older, Max would become an excellent soccer goalie and a great flag football player. Neither of these sports was open to girls at the high school level. So she tried out for basketball. Caroline became the star of the team. Max sat on the bench as she learned the game.

When ninth grade came around, Caroline went straight to the varsity. The girl in beige made the B-team. Marsha Leadman coached the B-team. Jill Boston coached varsity. Ms. Boston was a handsome woman that Max wanted to be like. Ms. Leadman and Ms. Boston were best friends, and so they decided that the B-team and varsity would practice together. Max and the varsity coach disagreed on how to play basketball. The girl in beige believed in using her whole body to do anything to get the ball, even if it meant she was on the floor, scrapping for the ball. Ms. Boston believed in something called poise. She saw the game as a kind of ballet, and she did not like how Max played ball. Consequently, the girl in beige sat on the bench for the next four years. She would daydream about her lucky break, but it never came.

There were coaches who appreciated the girl in beige's brand of ball. She met them at basketball camp each summer. If only she would move to their school district, they would say. She was considered one of the best ball handlers and defensive players at camp. Max loved camp. She loved the sweat on her brow and the sound of sneakers scraping on the floor. One year she and Beebee Sanders won the two-on-two competition. They even got a trophy for it. Still, Ms. Boston sat Max on the bench. Even though she sat on the bench, the girl in beige loved her bright red, clean, and crisp uniform. It was her favorite thing to wear. Max felt complete when she was wearing her uniform.

Finally, the girl in beige's stepmother, Ms. Waller, demanded an answer to why Max sat on the bench. It was the girl in beige's senior year, and Ms. Waller had seen her outshoot the boys in the backyard. Max's step-mother said she wanted an answer by supper as to why the girl in beige sat on the bench.

After school, Max tiptoed to the varsity coach's door. "Come in," said the voice on the other side of the door.

"My-my stepmother wants me to ask you why you don't play me," the girl in beige stuttered.

"I was thinking about cutting you this year."

A tear started down Max's face.

The coach continued. "Then I thought if I didn't play you this year you would quit. I guess I was wrong."

The girl in beige began to sob. *What kind of answer was that?* Max thought. *She was going to cut me!*

Ms. Boston would never appreciate the girl in beige's athletic ability, but Max would still look up to her basketball coach.

ALGEBRA

Boyd Crush was the best math teacher in the world. He usually only taught the higher mathematics, but he took on the girl in beige's beginning algebra class her ninth grade year. Mr. Crush could write on the board over his shoulder. He could look at one person and talk to another. He knew the answers to all the math problems instantly. But best of all, he called everybody Mr. and Miss. Max should have been called Miss Burke, but when Mr. Crush was calling the roll, he declared Maxine one of the prettiest names he had ever heard, and he therefore would call the girl in beige Maxine. Wow! This made her feel special.

The girl in beige took to algebra like a fish to water. She loved the subject. It all made sense. Mr. Crush would give extra bonus points on his tests, and Max always got them. So her test scores were 110 or 115, etc.

The math teacher had an idea that higher maths were not required to understand computer theory. So he taught all his classes the same math one month, and Max made the highest grades with some of the older students. Mr. Crush had proven his thesis.

The math teacher had a math contest, and Max won one of Mr. Crush's paintings, for he was a painter, not just a mathematician.

The girl in beige looked forward to a long and happy relationship with her math teacher, but he took another job the next year. He would be in charge of all math in another county. Max would wish Mr. Crush back, but it didn't work. She imagined him in her brain, only he never appeared again in real life.

To make things worse, the next year, she got one of the worst math teachers for geometry. Fortunately, geometry was easy to Max, and she ended up teaching the class how to do most of the problems. By teaching, she learned geometry, as well as algebra. But she missed Mr. Crush. She often wondered how his life ended up. Was he happy as an administrator, no longer in the classroom? Was he still painting? She would never know.

My Boy's Decline

After the divorce, My Boy got into drinking and drugs. He played loud music and went to a lot of parties. Max's brother got caught toilet papering the rival high school and ended up calling the daddy from jail. The girl in beige was both frightened of and frightened for her brother. My Boy was not selfish. He offered his sister a joint to smoke on numerous occasions. She turned him down every time.

Since the mama no longer lived in the house and the daddy was usually visiting girlfriends, My Boy could have as many friends over that he wanted and party to the maximum. The girl in beige missed the mama.

Max's brother worked at several different burger joints. He would lose his temper and walk off the job. My Boy could not tolerate stupidity. After high school he continued to party and get in trouble. The daddy told his only son that if he wasn't going to college, he needed to go into the service. My Boy chose the Air Force, where he found ways to continue to drink, do drugs, and get into trouble. It would be many years later, when he met his wife from Russia that My Boy would get straightened out.

Rocks and Minerals

The summer after ninth grade, the girl in beige took two courses at the local Science Center. One was a computer programming course with four other high school students. The other was a rock course with fifteen high school teachers getting credit for their Master's degree. It felt weird being with adults, but Max loved rocks. She knew all about the quartz and granite in the Charlotte area because she had collected and read about it since third grade. The girl in beige loved the way the cool rocks felt on her skin.

In the summer rock class, she learned the difference between minerals and rocks. A mineral is a solid material made of crystals. A rock is made up of more than one type of mineral. The professor gave each class member a collection of minerals and rocks. The minerals were numbered M1, M2, M3, etc. The M1 was on a tiny square of paper glued onto the mineral. M1 corresponded to a chart in the box holding the collection. The chart told the name of the mineral. The rocks were numbered R1, R2, R3, etc. They corresponded to their own chart. Max studied the rocks and minerals for hours each day that summer. She was totally mesmerized. The class also made their own crystals on a string and went on a field trip to find fossils and geodes. The girl in beige was in heaven. Max has long lost the charts, but she still has the minerals and rocks to this day. Some even have their original labels. Maybe someday, somebody will help her identify them again.

Acting Daddy

It was exciting having a father who was a professional actor and model. He was on commercials, in magazines, and on billboards. But best of all, he was in plays. From the time Max was age 10 until she was 17 the daddy took her to rehearsals, where actors called "line," when they forgot the words in the script. Sometimes they fell apart, saying they just couldn't learn it all by opening night. The girl in beige was there beside her father as he paced back and forth backstage just before the curtain came up. Some nights, she watched the play unfold just off stage. But most of the time, she sat in the audience.

One night in the restroom during intermission, a woman said to her friend, "That Brian Burke is good looking. I wish I could meet him." Max had Lila with her, aka My Baby, and they smiled at each other. When the play was over, they introduced the woman to the daddy. It made the lady's night.

The girl in beige was so close to her father that she never saw him as talented, though others told her so. She had to admit she was a bit scared when the daddy played a psychopath for a week. He was very convincing.

Musicals were the most fun of all. They sent a chill down Max's spine. There was nothing so amazing as a musical with singing and dancing that had looked like it would never make it in rehearsals but sparkled with pizzazz at show time.

After the plays, people would come backstage and congratulate the daddy. It impressed the girl in beige to see her father be so important. He was important at his day job as a computer programmer, but acting was so much more exciting.

The daddy liked to talk about his plays, and he included My Boy and Max in the conversations. It was these conversations that brought out the voice of the girl in beige.

The daddy had so much acting work that Max couldn't keep up with it. Other kids would say they saw her father on a billboard or in a commercial and catch her by surprise. One time her class went to see *A Midsummer Night's Dream,* and Amy read the program. "Hey, Max, did you know your father is in the play? He is one of the lovers."

"No, I had no idea."

Another time, the daddy invited his two oldest children to the movie set of *King.* It was the life story of Martin Luther king, Jr. Paul Winfield was playing Dr. King. Cicely Tyson played Mrs. King. The daddy played the mayor of one of the city in Alabama. The children were allowed on the set at a local courthouse, if they were quiet. But sometimes, they got bored and went outside the courtroom doors where local secretaries were peeking through the door windows.

The women were talking about the daddy.

One said, "Look at the man up there."

Another said, "He's good looking. Who is he?"

Seventeen-year-old My Boy popped up and offered, "That's my daddy!"

Max chuckled to herself.

The women had to go back to work, but they now knew that the actor they thought was good looking was a teenage boy's father.

The daddy's friends began to go to Hollywood, one by one. He went himself when Max went off to college, but he came back to take care of his ailing mother. He never acted again. Alcohol and depression won out.

HUGS

Todd Yang had a charismatic voice and good looks. He was the youth minister at the Baptist Church that Max had been a part of since first grade. The youth minister spoke with conviction in his voice of how much Jesus loved the youth, who were hanging onto Todd's every word. Todd backed up his talk with big bear hugs when he said, "I love you and so does Jesus." Consequently, the youth minister was always surrounded by teenagers. The girl in beige wasn't much of a hugger and was not drawn to crowds so she kept her distance from Todd. She preferred to sit next to Todd's wife Barbara during Wednesday night Bible study. Barbara had a dry wit and balanced Todd's upbeat attitude. The youth went on choir tours and retreats. All were fun and exciting. Max had a few people to hang around, Anna, Tammy, and Candice. So she wasn't always lonely. But none were close friends. They were more like friendly people she could sit with when she didn't sit next to Barbara.

Every Sunday night, there was something called Youth Fellowship. Twenty to thirty youth would invade yet another house and eat up all the food and play pool or just talk and finally settle down with Todd to sing songs about Jesus. The girl in beige usually walked around the houses until time to sing. She was fascinated with the different places in which church members lived.

When Todd pulled the bus into the church parking lot at the end of the evening, the youth minister had a ritual of hugging each person as they exited the bus. Max was scared of hugs, and she was pretty sure she was invisible. So she would attempt to slip past Todd while he was hugging somebody else. It never worked. A big hand would grab the back of the girl in beige's oversized t-shirt. Todd would pull Max into his arms and say, "Do you know how much I love you, Max? Jesus loves you even more!" And for a moment, the girl in beige didn't feel invisible at all.

CHOIR TOUR

The girl in beige was an alto who couldn't hear the music in her head. She relied on the girl next to her, who sang in Max's ear, to catch the notes. The church youth choir tour to Washington D.C. was a big event. It meant green pantsuit costumes for the girls and arm and leg movements that were hard to memorize. But best of all, it meant spending the night at church members' homes, all the way to D.C. and back. The girl in beige was captivated by the interior of the different houses. One of her favorite parts of choir tour was touring the variety of homes. There was nothing unusual about that.

What was strange about Max was that she took pictures of people's feet. Todd, the choir director, crossed his leg over his wife Barbara's leg and the girl in beige took a snapshot of the entangled feet. A group from the choir stretched out on the lawn with their feet in the air, after climbing the Washington monument. Max clicked away with all those toes in the still frame. The girl in beige had a hard time looking people in the eye, so she found expression in feet. It was much more comfortable for her.

CHURCH SOFTBALL

The girl in beige quit little league softball at the end of seventh grade because she had been spooked by her coaches. They smoked and cussed and lost most of their games. Max expected to get rid of these coaches, but they told her they were moving up with her and they would ask to have her on their team.

In the spring of the girl in beige's eleventh grade year, Anna, another church youth, asked Max if she wanted to play girl's church softball. The girl in beige had never considered church ball before this time, but it sounded like a good idea.

Max had grown in height and strength since she had played ball last. She had always played shortstop, but left field was what was open. She found that she could catch almost everything that came to the outfield, and her stronger arm had no problem throwing the softball to the infield. Even more exciting was her new batting power. She could hit homeruns! She also struck out a lot because she was swinging the bat so fast and so hard. But her homeruns balanced the strikeouts. What the girl in beige didn't know how to do was make friends on the team. The coaches were friendly, but she didn't know how to connect with her peers.

In one playoff game, Max had already hit a homerun and struck out twice. It was the bottom of the last inning, two were on base, and there were two outs. Her team was down by one run. The girl in beige walked up to the plate. "Strike one," called the umpire. Then there were two balls. Finally, Max connected. It was a homerun! The team was already celebrating when the girl in beige made it to first base. The two runners had touched home plate, and her team had won the game. Only, she didn't know how to join in the celebration. She stood frozen on the base and watched from afar. What was she missing that kept her away from people? What was it that made her feel alone in a crowd?

WHERE DO WE GO?

The girl in beige thought, *Where do all the lonely girls go? What happens when you don't want to be touched by other humans? Is there anything worse than this? I want to get close, but I can't. I watch from afar as everybody gives hugs. I don't know how to jump into the conversation. I'm definitely not cool. When we practice basketball, I feel close. I am in the middle. I wish my coach understood that I feel like I belong when I play ball. I liked it when I was little, and I played football with the boys. I like softball because I am so good at it that people smile at me. Only, when I hit homeruns, I don't know what to do. I stand off to the side and frown at their well wishes. I fear a hug is involved. I guess I can handle a pat on the back. Sometimes people don't know what to do with me. They feel my hesitation, and they step back and look at me funny. Oh, Jesus, are you the only one who understands me? Will I always be lonely?*

ALGEBRA TWO, TRIG, AND CALCULUS

Shirley Logic was as smart as Mr. Crush, but she was more serious. She would teach the girl in beige Algebra II her eleventh grade year, and trig and calculus her twelfth grade year. Max understood the first two maths with no difficulty, but calculus was different. She struggled with it.

The summer between eleventh and twelfth grades, Ms. Logic sent Max to a National Science Foundation Math Camp. It taught theories students wouldn't usually see until they were in college and, only then, if they were math majors. Just like in math class with Ms. Logic, some of the theories came easily, some came with difficulty.

There were times when Ms. Logic was not so serious, when she was with husband Sonny. Mr. and Mrs. Logic went with the National Honor Society to its convention at Jamison Island, Forida. The girl in beige and Sonny clicked right away. They both made the other laugh on the way to the convention. Sonny poked fun at Max for having relatives from one of the small town of in Alabama. Max entertained Sonny by counting dead animals on the highway.

Mr. and Ms. Logic also took the girl in beige and her friend Sonya to eat at one of the restaurants in Alabama. The resto had holes in the middle of the tables to throw away the peelings from all the boiled shrimp you wanted to eat.

The Logics gave Max help in applying to school. Ms. Logic thought the girl in beige should go to a small women's college like Lois Brown. The math teacher had been to Lois Brown, and she thought it would be a good fit for her student. Max wanted to go to Tech because it was cheaper. There was no money coming from home to go to college because the daddy lost his money in two divorces. So Ms. Logic had the entire calculus class fill out the one page application for Tech one day in class.

Her math teacher may have helped her get into the college of her choice, but Ms. Logic' intuition was right in that Max struggled at the big school. When Max finally switched to a small college, she took off with the help of a professor who cared about her, just as her high school teachers had.

THE MAN WHO HID BEHIND THE MAGAZINE

When he finished teaching the chemistry lesson each day, he expected his students to answer the corresponding questions at the end of each chapter. While the teenagers puzzled over the problems about molecules and the periodic table Richard Rizzo, known simply as Coach, would pick up his most recent copy of *Sports Illustrated* and hide behind the pages.

It didn't take the girl in beige very long to complete her chemistry assignment each day. Science and math flowed freely through her brain cells. She was gifted that way or perhaps the correct word was "haunted." It wasn't like she had chosen to have an analytic mind that flashed pictures of the correct answers forever in her head. And since the math and science pictures never left her internal theater, Max had become an A student, which pleased the daytime grownups called high school teachers.

One day after completing the questions at the end of the chapter, the A student glanced up to see some bad boys shooting paper wads into the waste basket next to the coach's desk. The coach was still absorbed in his magazine. Either he didn't notice the activity of the rowdy teens, or he was ignoring them while he lost himself in the articles he so loved.

Feeling a bit on the bored side of life, the girl in beige felt an urge to give trash basketball a try. So she stood up and tip toed over to the boys and asked if she could join in the fun. The bad boys kind of liked the idea of including an A student in their mischief. With smirks on their faces they handed Max a paper wad.

She aimed, and "whoosh," the first shot went in the can with ease. This made the rowdy boys grin their rowdy boy smiles. They handed the girl in beige another paper wad. She took aim once again. "Whoosh." She slammed the second shot in the waste basket. She was beginning to lose interest, but the bad boys laughed at the idea that a girl knew how to play their bad boy game. In a rare moment she would soon regret, Max succumbed to the peer pressure from the rowdy boys. She took the paper wad that was once again handed to her. Only this time, something possessed her hand.

With the flick of her wrist, the crunched up paper ball didn't soar towards the trash can. Instead the A student and the bad boys watched in horror as the paper wad flew toward the coach, who was still intent on his magazine. The paper wad popped the back of *Sports Illustrated* with a sickening smack before it slid off the desk next to the coach's feet.

Everybody scrambled to their seats. The girl in beige ducked behind the student in the desk in front of her, as if hiding would help in her moment of desperation.

The magazine in the coach's hands lowered in slow motion. A deep booming voice said, "Who threw that?" The bad boys pointed to Max, who was hiding her face in her arms. The coach muttered under his breath, "Max come here." The other students watched from the safety of their seats.

The walk to the coach's desk seemed eternal, as the A student considered the consequences of her actions. Would he send her straight to the principal's office or perhaps let her off with a lecture in the hall from the coach himself? The girl in beige felt extremely small the closer she got to the coach, who was many inches over six feet tall when he was standing. Fortunately, he remained seated. When she finally stood across from him, he whispered to her, "Come around to this side." Coach's desk was really a lab table, and so the trek around it took another painful 20 seconds to complete. Soon she was standing toe to toe with the man who hid behind the magazine. He said in a low voice so that only she could hear, "Pick it up and throw it in the trash and then go sit back down." Max disappeared behind the big lab table desk and picked up the paper wad that was right next to the coach's foot. She swallowed hard at being so close to the coach. She was terrified. With a trembling hand, she deposited the paper into the waste basket. When she returned to her seat, the girl in beige expected some form of punishment to follow. But it didn't come. Instead, the bell rang, and she realized the one called Coach was not going to lecture her or send her to the principal's office.

Forty years ago, a tall chemistry teacher gave Max's heart a sigh it had rarely known.

The next morning, as she walked to her locker, kids she didn't even know were approaching the A student and exclaiming, "You threw a paper wad at Coach Rizzo and didn't get in trouble. That is so awesome!" For a day she was popular for something she wished she had never done.

After that day, Max acted like the A student that she was.

She didn't grow closer or farther away from the coach. She was just another student in his class, she thought.

Then in the spring, the man who hid behind the magazine asked to see Max in the hall. The girl in beige couldn't figure out what she had done wrong.

In the hall, Max studied her super comfortable, red suede ProKeds basketball sneakers.

Coach Rizzo opened his mouth and said, "I want you to take advanced chemistry next year. I will be teaching it for the first time, and I want you in my class."

Max was puzzled. Advanced chemistry was fourth period, the same time as basketball class. Coach knew this and said, "She isn't going to play you. I'll tailor this class around you."

The girl in beige never looked up at the tall coach. She just grunted an affirmative and went to the counselor's office to change her schedule.

Max didn't quite understand it then, but it seemed the coach liked her. This was more than a person who thought of herself as nobody, could imagine.

THE STEPMOTHER

The girl in beige's father married Liz Waller the spring of Max's junior year. Ms. Waller was a good looking actress and model. The daddy was smitten by her beauty. The couple divorced the next fall, but not before Max felt the impact of another adult in her life.

Ms. Waller was fanatical about cleanliness. She demanded a bright and shining house inside and out. That meant a spotless kitchen, walls scrubbed on the stairwell, and leaves swept off the eternal driveway. One evening, her stepmother said the girl in beige had to clean her room before she went to a movie with her father. Max felt like a visitor in someone else's room, for her bedroom was too big and had a lot of strange furniture. The girl in beige preferred small and cozy with only a small bed and dresser. She was commanded to clean this lonely foreign land. Max cleaned and cleaned. So father and daughter were off to the movies. Just before the movie began, Ms. Waller came into the theater to drag out the girl in beige. Her father escorted the stepmother to the parking lot where they had a fight over the dust bunnies Max had left under her bed. The girl in beige didn't even know such creatures existed.

In the summer, after math camp, Ms. Waller said her stepdaughter had to get a job. To the local fast food Max went to become a cashier. When school started, she was still working, plus taking trig, A.P. Calculus, physics, Advanced Chemistry, and A.P. English. When she fell asleep in calculus, Ms. Logic wrote a note and demanded the job be ended. And it was.

When the girl in beige got sick or had a doctor's appointment, it was Ms. Waller who volunteered to come and pick her up. Max wanted her father, but he sent his wife instead. The third time Ms. Waller picked up the girl in beige, the stepmother said accusingly, "You never thank me!"

Max remembered thanking Ms. Waller the two times before. The only reason she hadn't said anything the third time was because she was so sick. The girl in beige just cried in response to the accusation. She had nothing to say.

Max's stepmother could not believe the baggy clothes the girl in beige was wearing, so she took her shopping. Ms. Waller had Max undress to her bra and panties while the store attendants brought her clothes to try on. The girl in beige was a very modest person and felt naked in front of the strangers and the stepmother. It was a very difficult situation for Max. According to Ms. Waller, the girl in beige had to wear a dress every Friday. The first Friday just happened to be Halloween when everybody else was wearing costumes. On her way to Advanced Chemistry, Coach Nealson, the Earth Science teacher next door to Coach Rizzo, fell on the floor screaming. "What's wrong?" asked one of his students bending over Coach Nealson.

"Max Burke is wearing a dress!" yelled out the coach. Of course the girl in the dress was mortified. She was not going to cry. She marched past Coach Rizzo and took her seat and put her head on her desk. Coach Rizzo approached and whispered in her ear as gently as possible, "You look good."

Ugh! Thought the girl in beige.

That evening was the school's Halloween carnival with a costume contest. Ms. Waller had given Max what she thought would make a great Raggedy Ann costume. The red wig was unkempt and the tennis dress was too tight. So Max went into the attic and found red fish net stockings and a small red purse. She went to the carnival as a hooker. Some people didn't even recognize her. But best of all, she won the costume contest. The girl in beige never told her stepmother.

JOGGING

With the stepmother came three stepsiblings all younger than Max. Two of the stepsiblings lived with Ms. Waller: June and Alan. June was thin like her mother. She played the album from the movie *Grease* over and over again.

When the girl in beige was in eleventh grade, June decided that she and the girl in beige would jog, not run, in NC's Fourth of July, 10K, Cotton Road Race. Ten kilometers is 6.2 miles. Max had never jogged over two miles. She ran laps around the gym for basketball practice. But she rarely jogged just to jog. June changed that.

First the daddy had to take the girl in beige to get running shoes. They were yellow and called waffle trainers.

On the actual jogging days, June and Max did three warm-up stretches the running store had recommended. The neighborhood they lived in was gorgeous. The stepmother owned a mansion in the Elwood area. The two girls jogged past giant manicured lawns with long driveways and houses set way back from the curb. Each day the girls got stronger and jogged a little further. The girl in beige didn't particularly like jogging. In fact she found it boring. But she liked her stepsister's company, and she liked getting in shape. After they jogged, they did three cool-down stretches. These exercises were different from the warm-up stretches at the beginning of the jog. One of the cool-down stretches was walking on heels. People in cars would slow down and ask if the girls needed a ride because they looked like they were injured when they walked on their heels.

The stepsisters had to wake up early the day of the race. NC is very hot in the summer, so the race is in the early morning, to prevent heat exhaustion. Max and June were placed in the last section of the giant pack of runners. They had said they could run ten minute miles. The girl in beige had not run over five miles, and so she wasn't even sure she could finish the 6.2 miles race to get a t-shirt.

The crowd that would cheer the racers on was overflowing. There was so much energy from the other joggers and from the cheering crowd. There was a special thrill that this was a one of a kind special event.

About half way through the race, Max pulled ahead of her stepsister. She continued the race, surrounded by strangers. The daddy and the stepmother were in the crowd on the side of the road and called out loud enough for the girl in beige to see them. She was even more determined to finish the race. Sweat poured down Max's face, and she had a stitch in her side. But the crowd cheered on her and her fellow runners, "You are near the end! Keep going!" Finally she jogged across the finish line. The girl in beige claimed her prized race t-shirt. The stepmother hugged her when they met up. She had done it! Max was a veteran of the Cotton Road Race. A few minutes later, June also finished the race, received a hug from her mother and found the t-shirt table.

A few months later, June and Max's parents separated permanently. June and her brother Alan peered out through the screen door as the girl in beige and the daddy pulled out of the driveway to never return. It broke Max's heart to leave behind her stepsiblings. She had grown fond of them, but she would hardly ever see them again.

LONELINESS

The girl in beige saw people on dates and in couples all around her in high school. She went on one date her senior year. It was a mistake. The boy, a junior, was in her Advanced Chemistry class. He asked her out right in front of Coach Rizzo. Max was confused as what to do. She didn't want to appear as a loser to the coach, so she said, "Yes." She regretted it right away because she wasn't attracted to the boy. In fact she wasn't attracted to any boy or any girl. Her sex drive was delayed. The girl in beige went on the date anyway and was miserable when the boy put his arm around her. After that catastrophe, Max was pretty sure she would end up a lonely old maid.

She listened to the Beatles' "Eleanor Rigby" that asked, "All the lonely people, where do they all come from?" She also listened to the band America that had a song simply called "Lonely People" in which they sang, "This is for all the lonely people..." And the Electric Light Orchestra had a song titled "Telephone Line" where nobody picks up the telephone, and the singer is left all alone. These songs fueled the loneliness that already flamed inside the girl in beige. She would put her headphones on and listen to her music for hours.

A.P. English

Max signed up for Advanced Placement English for the challenge, not for the A.P. test at the end of the year. The class was taught by Marsha Leadman. Ms. Leadman had a gruff exterior that the girl in beige had known when she was Max's basketball coach in eighth and ninth grades. Ms. Leadman also had a deep, stern voice and she mooed. According to Max's brother, mooing is when a person says, "Hmm," in a deep voice. To make things even more frightening to the girl in beige, her lower locker was right next to Ms. Leadman's door. This meant that each day, Ms. Leadman gently kicked the locker door to get Max to say hello to her. Intimidated, the girl in beige mumbled a hello.

But in class, the teacher with the stern voice was a surprising delight. She found it a joy to be working with some of the smartest kids in the school. And Max, who was slow to read the books did remarkably well picking out themes to some of the greatest stories of all time. Ms. Leadman was very pleased.

On Valentine's Day, Ms. Leadman asked her students to pull their chairs into a circle. As usual, the girl in beige tried to avoid sitting next to the stern-voiced teacher. Even with all the good that had taken place in the classroom, Max was still very much intimidated by Ms. Leadman. But the ploy of the girl in beige did not work this time. Ms. Leadman waited for all the students to pull into the circle before she squeezed in next to Max.

The stern voiced teacher asked everybody to write a Valentine's poem. The girl in beige wrote something goofy because she felt goofy writing about affection of any kind. Then Ms. Leadman asked everybody to pass his or her poem to the left. This meant Ms. Leadman's poem ended up on Max's desk.

At first the girl in beige just stared at the folded over piece of paper. "Read it," whispered the stern-voiced teacher.

So Max opened it and read, "Roses are red. Violets are blue. I just wanted you to know that I really like you."

The girl in beige sat frozen, staring at her desk the rest of the period. Ms. Leadman asked to see her after class. *Oh, Lord*, thought Max.

Ms. Leadman said in her stern voice, "I really do like you. You'll just have to deal with it."

The girl in beige studied her red suede ProKeds. "Yes, Ma'am," She mumbled, before scurrying out the door.

From then on, Ms. Leadman went back to her gruff exterior, except when she was having fun in class. But Max knew this cool tough woman liked her, and it felt good to the girl in beige.

Unfortunately, Max had a small vocabulary. Because she sounded so informed when she discussed the theme of a book, Ms. Leadman didn't know it. But it was evident to the girl in beige when she took the Advanced Placement test, that she didn't understand most of the questions. This meant she did poorly on the test and Ms. Leadman was upset. Max was ashamed of her limited vocabulary, so she never explained to her teacher why she failed the A.P. test. This did not affect her grade in the class. She had performed so well in class that Max got As from Ms. Leadman.

RAKING YARDS

During basketball practice, a redheaded girl named Sonya asked if she could be Max's friend. No one had ever asked that before. Amy and Caroline were more like protective sisters who had other close friends. But Sonya wanted to spend time with the girl in beige. The red headed girl was smart, athletic, and witty like Max. The difference was that Sonya pressed her t-shirts and blue jeans, which was quite different from the rag-tag look of the girl in beige. Sonya also had a brand new, silver Camero. They would drive around to different teacher's houses to visit.

The main person they visited was Ms. Logic, the math teacher, and her husband Sonny. The Logics liked to work on their yard. They saw the girls' unexpected visits as welcomed help, and the girls saw the opportunity to help as a wonderful way to visit with one of their favorite teachers. As a reward, the Logics would take the girls out for lunch. The math teacher and her husband were very witty and a delight to be with.

Sonya and Max decided to spread their good cheer. They offered to rake the yard of their school counselor, Mr. Moore. He happily agreed and also was a delight with which to eat lunch.

When Caroline heard what they were doing, she begged the duo to offer to help Ms. Leadman, the A.P. English teacher, with her leaves. The reason she wanted this task was because she admired Ms. Boston, the basketball coach. Ms. Boston and Ms. Leadman were best friends, who lived down the street from one another. So if they offered to rake Ms. Leadman's leaves, then Ms. Boston would be there. As they began the gigantic task, Ms. Leadman said to Max, "You are with me. I rake, and you bag." The girl in beige knew better than to argue with the stern-voiced English teacher.

Lunch was awkward, with Max intimidated by Ms. Leadman and Caroline in awe of Ms. Boston. Sonya carried their end of the conversation. No one noticed the lack of talking on the part of Max and Caroline. They had never talked much to their coach and teacher before, so it wasn't expected they talk much at lunch.

The girl in beige pondered Ms. Leadman choosing her, and it felt good in her heart.

BEING SEEN

In the summer between eleventh and twelfth grades, Max bought a t-shirt that said "NOBODY" on it. It captured how she felt invisible most of the time.

She started advanced chemistry in the fall, just as she had promised Coach Rizzo, and he started a strange ritual after lunch each day. The girl in beige would hang out with the popular group that included Sonya, Caroline, and Amy. She barely listened to the conversation around her. Coach Nealson, the earth science teacher, and Coach Rizzo would walk down the hall from lunch back to their classrooms. Coach Nealson was an outgoing man who waved hello to everybody he knew. Coach Rizzo was much more particular. When they arrived at the popular group, Coach Nealson would begin his hellos, for there were many. Coach Rizzo on the other hand had one hello.

"Hello, Max," he would say.

The girl in beige would study her toes, as usual. "Uh, hello," she would mumble back. She didn't understand how the coach could see her when so few could see her outside the classroom. Sure, she was known as an A student, but otherwise she was nobody.

Coach acted even stranger at football games. Max loved football games because it meant a cool breeze on her skin and the drum corp playing a lengthy piece after each game. Oh, how she loved the percussion. As the drums sounded out their song, Coach Rizzo and the football team boarded the bus. Coach had become the head coach of the football team the girl in beige's senior year. After each team member and the other coaches loaded up, it was Coach Rizzo's turn to get on the bus. But just before he got on, he looked through the crowd in the direction of the drum corp. Finally, he found who he sought.

"Hello, Max," he would call over the music and wave.

The girl in beige would grimace and wave back.

"Why does he do that?" asked the girl next to Max.

"I don't know," she mumbled back.

INCIDENTS

Before Max could enter Coach Rizzo's classroom, he required that she look up from her books that were slipping out of her hand and say hello. Coach Rizzo and Coach Nealson waited between classes outside their doors that were next to each other. They usually kept a running conversation, but Coach Rizzo would stop the conversation when Max arrived, tripping over her untied shoe laces on her red ProKed sneakers.

"Hello, Max."

Max kept her head lowered and moved toward the doorway.

The man who hid behind the magazine would step in her way. "This is when you say hello back."

"Hello," the girl in beige mumbled.

Coach didn't move from the doorway. "Now look me in the eye and say it."

Max slowly, painfully looked at the tall man. "Hello," she mumbled yet again.

"Good enough. You can pass."

One day, the girl in beige decided she didn't want to look anybody in the eye. She had observed another kid trying to show the man who hid behind the magazine a worm. Coach seemed uncomfortable. So on the day that Max didn't want to look anybody in the eye, she approached Coach with a closed fist. "Here." He opened his hand to receive the present. "It's a worm," she announced as she opened her hand. Coach Rizzo jumped away and yelled. The girl in beige's eyes opened wide. There was no worm. She had been kidding. But she had made the coach jump and yell. It made her heart feel very bad.

If she was wondering if the coach forgave her, she didn't have to wait long. She dropped a test tube during lab one day. It broke to pieces. After cleaning up the mess, she walked the long walk to his desk. As usual, Coach was reading a magazine. "I dropped a test tube." She said to the back of *Sports Illustrated*.

"Uh huh," came the reply. The girl in beige knew that when the boy across the lab table had dropped something, the coach had yelled at him and demanded he pay for it. So she stood there, waiting to be yelled at and to find out how much she owed.

Coach could still feel her presence. He put down the magazine. "Yes?"

"How much do I owe?"

"Nothing."

"Nothing?"

"Nothing."

"Oh."

Yet again she was perplexed by his grace towards her.

Another day, Sonya, who sat behind Max, whispered, "Do you want a chocolate bar?"

"No," the girl in beige whispered back, for she knew that candy was strictly forbidden in Coach Rizzo's classroom.

"Here." Sonya placed the bar in Max's hand. "You won't get in trouble. You never do."

Coached approached the girl in beige. "What do you have in your hand?"

She opened her hand to expose the Snickers bar.

"Open it."

Max peeled off the wrapper. Her hands were shaking.

"Now hand it to me."

She handed Coach the candy.

He took a big bite. Almost half the bar was gone.

"Thanks," said the coach, after he had finished eating his bite and had handed the rest to the girl in beige. Coach Rizzo walked back to his desk.

"Told you," whispered Sonya.

And Max looked at the coach for a long time, wondering what she had done to deserve his favor.

When the class had to do unknowns, the girl in beige quivered a little. What if she couldn't guess all the ingredients in her test tube? She had done fine in practice, but this was now a week-long test. Her guesses didn't go well, and Max feared she would fail.

The next week, the students returned to have Coach tell them three students had forgotten to turn in the number of their unknown. The girl in beige was one of them. *Oh no,* she thought, *I failed.* For the coach had warned that not turning in your number meant automatic failure. It was with that number that the coach knew what was in the test tube.

The coach continued, "I have decided to give each of you an A."

Huh.

He did it again, thought Max. *How do I deal with this? How do I deal with somebody being so nice to me. Oh, my god.*

Max's little sister took advanced chemistry four years later. She said, "I don't see what you see in Coach Rizzo. He isn't nice at all. He flunked a lot of people when we did the unknown."

And there she had it, proof that the man who hid behind the magazine had been extra nice to her, and she would just have to accept it.

WISHING FOR ANOTHER LIFE

Max thought, *Sometimes I wish I could go live with Coach Rizzo and his wife. They would see me for who I am and not be too busy to be with me. I heard that they did take in another kid because his parents kicked him out. I'm not that lucky. My parents want me. They even fight over me, since they are divorced. But the mama is busy with her gifted kids she teaches and with local politics she fights and her church library where she spends all her extra time. And the daddy is busy with acting and girlfriends. We hardly see either one of them. When we do, they are tired. The daddy doesn't come home.*

My brother gets in a lot of trouble these days. He can't protect me from the world. My baby sister has gone to live with the mama. They have moved to an apartment in another part of town. Does anybody see my pain? I feel so lonely, and I don't know how to explain it to anyone. So in my mind, I go to Coach Rizzo's house, and we sit down to supper and have conversations, and he and his wife smile at me and say they are glad that I am with them.

SCARY THINGS

Just like when she was little, the girl in beige was afraid of being kidnapped by a stranger. It scared her to her very core. Max felt invisible and thought no one would miss her. She would be lost forever.

The girl in beige was also afraid of Halloween. The scary costumes felt real. She did not like opening the door to strangers in the dark. It spooked her. Max would never outgrow her fear of Halloween.

Worst of all, the girl in beige could not watch scary movies. She knew this without having to go see them. But Sonya was going to see *Amityville Horror* with some friends that she sang with in a chorus. She begged Max to come. Against her better judgment, the girl in beige went. *Amityville Horror* is a true story about a family terrorized by strange manifestations in a house that was the site of a grisly mass murder. Max felt like she was right there in the real haunted house. She was unable to remind herself that it was a just a movie. Sonya took the girl in beige home to the daddy. The daddy felt sorry for his daughter and tried to comfort her. She was absolutely petrified. Max stayed up that night scared the demonic forces from the movie were going to kidnap her and take her to hell.

To this day, she stays away from horror picture shows as much as possible.

THE COUNSELOR

Mr. Moore had been the girl in beige's academic counselor since eighth grade, but it wasn't until twelfth grade that she really got to know him. For one, he liked Snicker's chocolate bars and enjoyed when Max and Sonya brought him one. They could count on a good visit when they brought him the candy present. He would chew on the bar, and they would fill him in on all their classes.

Her mother called the counselor because she felt Max's stepmother was too hard on her daughter. So Mr. Moore rescued the girl in beige and took her to his house for the day.

As a graduation gift, Max's stepfather, called Mr. P., decided to make her 100 meatballs. The girl in beige could invite anybody she wanted to eat the scrumptious treat. She chose Sonya and Mr. Moore. They both were very thankful for the invite because the meatballs were beyond description in taste. That's what kind of person the counselor was, someone Max felt comfortable inviting over for a meal.

The last thing Mr. Moore did for Max was take her down the street to the local Masonic lodge to apply for a scholarship for college. By then, her father had divorced her stepmother and lost a lot of money in the process. There just wasn't any money for college, so Mr. Moore stepped in and found the Masonic lodge scholarship which helped a great deal. Max also won the Beta Club scholarship. She figured Mr. Moore had a hand in that, too. Between the two scholarships, Max was able to pay for her first year of college.

Good academic counselors are hard to find. The girl in beige was lucky to have hers.

GRADUATION INVITATION

When it came time for graduation, the girl in beige knew she wanted the man who hid behind the magazine to be there. So Sonya drove her to the coach's house, and they slipped an invitation in his mailbox.

The next day, Coach Rizzo said he had another obligation and he would not be able to make graduation. Max was sorely disappointed. Coach tried to make up for it with a graduation card that kidded that the girl in beige must have bribed her teachers. It also had a homemade pretend gift certificate to Joe's Army Surplus for more fatigues. The girl in beige didn't realize Coach Rizzo was so creative.

Pig Pickin'

When the girl in beige graduated from high school, she and her mother drove to Aunt June's in South Carolina. Cousin Jason and his siblings decided to throw a pig pickin' to celebrate Penny and Max's departure from mainstream education. The pig was roasted all night and all day, before it was ready. Parents were not invited to the party.

Everybody drank alcohol at the pig pickin'. Jack Daniel's whiskey mixed with Mountain Dew soft drink was the poison of choice. The girl in beige had never had alcohol before. The Mountain Dew made the whiskey easy to swallow, and so she drank up.

One of Penny's neighbors called Max over and offered her a marijuana cigarette. She had never smoked a joint before, but that didn't stop her accepting the offer. And so it went, booze and drugs, until the girl in beige climbed up on a car hood and started yelling like Tarzan. She could not shut up. Eventually, Jason talked her down, escorted her inside the house, and planted Max in front of the TV set. "You cannot come back to the party," Jason proclaimed. The girl in beige felt disappointed and angry for being barred from the fun, but she respected and feared Jason enough not to cross him. After her cousin went back to the party, Max kept grinning and giggling at the drama on the television. If the mama and Aunt June suspected anything, they never said it.

The next day, the girl in beige was ashamed of her behavior from the night before, but she didn't say anything to anyone.

SHE'S HIDING UNDER THE TABLE: ONE WOMAN'S LIFE WITH ASPERGER'S AND DEPRESSION

PART FOUR – THE YOUNG WOMAN IN BLUE

YOUNG WOMAN IN BLUE

The daddy gave seventeen-year-old Max some money to buy pants for college. She bought two pair of corduroys for the price of one pair of jeans. One pair of pants was maroon, and the other was blue. Max fell in love with the blue pair and wore them almost every day. During her college years, Max was the young woman in blue.

The daddy helped the young woman in the new corduroy pants move into her dorm room at Tech. She was a mathematics major. Although she had lived in NC most of her life and was living in NC, not far away from home, Max was scared to death. She had rarely been on her own away from the daddy, except to be with more family, like Aunt June and Aunt Lydia. She had also been to Washington D.C. with the patrols and on choir tour. But that had been one week at a time, not three months that make up a quarter at college. When the daddy left, the young woman in blue felt very alone and started to cry. An hour later, Sonya, who had raked leaves with Max in high school, appeared at her door. She had just moved into the dorm next door. Max wasn't so lonely after that. Sonya helped the young woman in blue start her new adventure. There were classes and new people to meet and more classes and new food to try and more classes.

COLLEGE CHEMISTRY

First quarter chemistry at Tech was hard. The young woman in blue made Cs on the tests because she couldn't remember the formulas and equations. There was a test every week, which meant another C. Fortunately, the lab component was easy. It had unknowns to figure out, like Coach Rizzo had taught Max in high school.

For the final exam, the students were allowed to write anything they wanted on a three by five card. The young woman in blue was happy with this. Professor Elexor said the exam could count all to nothing, depending on how it helped your grade. So if Max made better than a C, the final exam grade would be her final grade. If she made less than a C, the exam counted nothing.

Dr. Elexor didn't post his grades on his door like other professors. Students had to meet with him in person. This terrified the young woman in blue. Looking at her shoes, she shuffled into the professor's office and took a seat.

"My name is Max Burke," the young woman managed to get out.

"Ah, Miss Burke! I've been waiting for you. You ruined my curve. Where have you been hiding all quarter?" Professor Elexor wore thick-rimmed glasses and a pressed, white lab jacket. His black hair was slicked down.

Petrified Max peeked at the professor.

"You see," continued Dr. Elexor, "you made the second highest grade on the exam out of class of 135. What do you have to say for yourself?"

The young woman in blue said nothing.

The professor didn't seem to notice. "My only conclusion is that you are lazy, and I refuse to give somebody like you an A in my class. That means you ruined the curve for all the people beneath you. I'm giving you a B for the quarter."

I made a B! All right! I made a B.

Dr. Elexor may have thought he was penalizing the young woman, but she was so happy to get a B instead of a C. And in her heart, she knew she really earned an A.

College English

Every freshman had to take English 101. It was one of the ways Tech kept up with how its first years were doing in the tough environment. English was one of the rare small classes and every new student had to meet with his or her professor to check on how the student was doing psychologically. It was joked that the classwork came so fast at Tech that it was like turning on a fire hydrant. One in three students would flunk out by the end of the first year. Another third would flunk out their second year.

English 101 was also the place where the five paragraph essay was taught. The first paragraph introduces the middle three paragraphs. The middle three paragraphs each take a different direction on the main topic. The last paragraph summarizes the middle three paragraphs. The five-paragraph essay was necessary for the North Carolina Regents exam that all college students had to take to prove they could write.

When it was time for Max to meet with the English professor, it was the middle of the term. He had a good idea about her writing. She was terrified to be seen by this man, so she did her usual looking at her toes, as if they were interesting.

"Come in. Come in. I'm so glad to finally be meeting with you," the English professor said, in an unusually cheerful voice. Most of Tech professors were serious types. This Professor was young and full of energy. "What should I call you, Maxine or Max?"

"Max," the young woman mumbled.

"Okay, Max, you are a genius. I've never had a student like you before, someone who understands the material so well. You must be making all A's."

The young woman in blue wasn't making all A's but she wasn't going to argue.

"Listen. If you rewrite your last essay, you will be the first student to whom I will give an A."

"Huh?"

"Yes, that's how good you are, just one essay away from an A."

Max rewrote the essay, but she was new at writing the five-paragraph essay. She got a B at the end of the term, but she couldn't forget that a professor thought she was a genius, when it came to picking out themes and understanding authors.

THE KIND YOUNG WOMAN

Cassiopeia (Cassie) House was named for a constellation in the sky. She was the counselor, or resident advisor, on Sonya's hall. Sonya was the young woman who had raked leaves in high school with Max. Cassie was a kind young woman who would do anything for her friends. Max moved to the hall the next quarter and lived next door to Cassie. Cassie was so smart that she started Tech in her senior year of high school. Her last year of high school and her first year at Tech were the same year. The kind young woman was also an athlete. She made the Tech softball team and was the quarterback on the dorm's intramural flag football team.

In Max's second year, Cassie got promoted from resident advisor to being in charge of two dorms. Max became an R.A. under Cassie. It was during this time that the young woman in blue came to talk to the kind young woman. Max talked to Cassie more than she had anybody else in the past. Granted, it was mostly monologues about herself, on the young woman in blue's part. But she was talking! Cassie was a patient listener who interjected her own thoughts, when she could get a word in the conversation. Max and the kind young woman would lie on the floor of Cassie's apartment with their feet up on the sofa and talk about the concerns of the universe. The young woman in blue talked to Cassie because she had respect for the kind young woman, and Cassie seemed truly interested in what Max had to say. Not very many people really wanted to hear what the young woman in blue had to say. It didn't bother a lot of people that Max said so little.

The kind young woman was a great cook and often invited other friends to eat. One evening, she put on a big spread for Ray, a man from Max's church whom the young woman in blue talked about a lot. Ray had wanted to meet Max's school friends because the young woman in blue talked about her friends to him. It felt kind of weird for Max to have two parts of her life meet. But overall the dinner was enjoyable because Cassie and Ray kept up the conservation and the young woman in blue didn't have to say much. Although Max was getting better at one to one talking, groups still baffled her.

The young woman in blue would often forget to feed herself. It just wasn't something she thought about or planned for the week. Cassie would pick up the slack and feed her friend. Her kindness was very much appreciated by Max.

DROWN PROOFING

"Number five, don't disappoint me again!"

Drown-proofing was a requirement at Tech. The young woman in blue had learned to tread water, swim under water, and do the back stroke above water by the time she took the class. But she was terribly afraid of deep water. When the swim coach took roll each day, the students stood under their assigned numbers. Max was number five. She was one of three young women in the class. The other twenty students were young men. The coach couldn't understand Max's problem. She had the body of an athlete, but she chickened out of the assignments. The first assignment was to have your feet tied behind your back and to tread water for a half an hour. The young woman in blue freaked out and asked to get out of the pool. She cried all the way back to her dorm and asked the daddy to come and get her. He calmed her down and told her she would do better next time. He was right. Max passed the foot-tied test the next time she tried it. But she missed a lot of tests here and there except for the absolutely required ones. If she passed all the required tests, she would proudly make a C in the class. There was plenty of extra credit to get an A, but number five was too afraid to try for extra points. This was not good enough for the coach, and so he refused to learn her name. She got used to hearing, "Oh, number five, not again."

Max had to pass hands tied behind the back and then both hands and feet tied. The ropes represented tangled clothes. The young woman in blue barely made it, but she did it. She passed. Next was the hour swim where the class had to swim with their clothes on. The coach told her to do the backstroke and another student told her to wear painter pants because they were made of the lightest material. She listened to the advice, and she passed that test too.

The last test was the hardest. It was called the underwater swim, and no one could pass the entire class without passing the underwater swim. The students had to jump off the high dive, do a flip underwater, and not resurface until they swam underwater the length of an Olympic sized pool up and back. To barely pass, you could resurface halfway back after swimming the first link. In other words ¾ of the test got a passing grade. The coach said it was a thinking test. It was all in their heads.

There was a chance they would run out of oxygen. In that case, the body would shut down the conscious mind but would keep swimming. If the coach saw someone swim into the wall, it meant his or her brain was shutting down. He would send his swim team helpers to grab the person out of the water. According to the coach, the person would have an emotional reaction when they came back to consciousness, either happy or mad. But the coach assured the students that running out of oxygen rarely happened. It wasn't something to worry about. Number five hopped to the back of the line.

The first person in line was a fifteen-year-old genius with a tiny body. The whole class watched him jump, flip underwater, and then swim up and back, only he didn't stop swimming. Sure enough he had run out of oxygen. The swim team assistants grabbed him and pulled him out of the water. His teeth were clenched shut, and his body was screaming an ungodly sound because it couldn't get any oxygen. His body had shut his mouth to keep the water from getting in. Now it had to be pried open to get the oxygen in. Finally, the young man woke up and started laughing.

"Wow. What a high! I passed!" The coach had told the class if you started to feel really good under the water it could mean you were running out of oxygen. The whole class felt uneasy. The coach reassured them that it wouldn't happen again.

The class began to pass the test one by one with no unusual events. That is until the tenth young man ran out of oxygen. And he wasn't small. His body sounded like it was dying as it screamed for oxygen. But they couldn't get his mouth open at first. Not only was he in agony, so was the class witnessing the whole thing. Finally, the assistants opened the young man's mouth.

He woke up and was very angry. "Why did that happen to me?"

"You passed," reassured the coach. Still the coach claimed this was a quirk. And so the class started swimming up and down again with no event. Finally, it was number five's turn. Her eyes were big.

"Don't mess this up, number five," taunted the coach.

Max's entire body was trembling as she climbed the high dive. She jumped and flipped and swam the length of the pool. She turned around and half way back she started to feel a high. *Uh-oh*, she thought. *I will not run out of oxygen.* So she resurfaced, only she couldn't move or talk.

"Get her," yelled the coach. Two young men jumped in the pool and dragged number five to the side. "Oh, number five, how do you do it? You swam the least amount, and yet you made it back to the halfway point so I have to pass you."

She had passed the test and the course!

The next year, drown proofing was no longer required. It was considered too dangerous. But the young woman in blue was glad she took it and passed. She had accomplished feats she never knew she could do. The coach was wrong. Number five was not a goof off; she was a success.

PAJAMA PARTY

Max's girls' dorm and one of the boys' dorms decided to have a pajama party. The girls would supply the food, the boys the drink. The drinking age was still age 18, so the drinks were legal. At the party, the young woman in blue wore a long, blue robe that zipped up the front. She ate a lot and drank a lot. She had not had a lot to drink before that evening except at the pig pickin' at Aunt June's house. Soon, Max could barely stand up. That was when Rex approached her. One of the young woman's friends told her that Rex had been interested in her for about a month. Apparently, the party gave him the courage to talk to Max.

"Do you want to go to my room?"

"Sure." said the drunk, young woman in blue.

He took her hand, and they stumbled to his room.

They kissed for a while until Rex said, "Do you want to do it?"

"Do what?" asked Max, not in tune to what was going on.

"You know...IT!"

"OH! NO! NO, I don't," the young woman in blue barely made it to her feet. She had to go.

Rex tried to coax her back into the room by taking her hands in his.

Max pushed the young man backwards, and he landed sitting down. The young woman in blue made her exit and made it out of the dorm just before she threw up on the ground outside.

The next day, Rex apologized for being so forward, and Max accepted his apology, but she would not go out with him. She didn't feel that way. The urge to have sex made no sense to her. Rex glared at Max when he saw her around the campus. But the young woman in blue didn't know how to explain her panic when somebody was attracted to her. She didn't know how to explain that her hormones had not caught up with her age.

Painting Dorms

Clarissa Phelps was like a force of nature. She showed up in Max's dorm room at the beginning of the second/winter quarter and announced, "I told your new roomie to switch with me. I decided I wanted you as my roommate. I saw you in chemistry. Hi, I'm Phelps. That's my last name. I'll call you Burke."

Phelps and Burke got along quite well. Phelps found them a bunk bed. Max was relegated to the top. Phelps had a way of arguing one side of an argument one day and the other side the next day. She especially liked to argue with the news. Phelps also ate spaghetti almost every day to save money. Probably the most distinctive personality trait of Burke's roommate was her trickster ways. She loved to giggle with glee. Phelps poured a bucket of cold water on Cassie when the counselor was in the shower. Phelps told Max there was something wrong with the top of the blinds in the window above Burke's desk, and Max was wearing only her cut off t-shirt and her panties. There was nothing wrong with the blinds, but a crowd of people waiting on the bus outside the dorm got to see Burke's near naked body. They cheered.

Argh! thought the young woman in blue. But Burke couldn't stay mad at Phelps for long. By bedtime she found her roommate clever and even saw the humor of someone like herself, shy with her body, showing off to a crowd.

Phelps's mother worked for the housing office at Tech. She got Phelps and Burke great jobs painting the dorms all summer. Usually only juniors and seniors got the job. The roomies were put together as a finishing team. That meant they brushed the windows and ceiling and corners. Phelps was fast. Burke was a perfectionist. They were a great team. But most of all, they got to talk and make money while they talked. Talking to Phelps and getting to know each other better felt good in Burke's heart.

There was also plenty of overtime, so Max made enough money to pay for the next school year. It made her happy to provide for herself.

R.O.T.C.

Max joined Air Force R.O.T.C. the spring/third quarter of her first year at Tech. It was a possible way to pay for school her junior and senior years if she signed on the dotted line. The dotted line meant four years in the Air Force after college. The young woman in blue wasn't sure she was ready to commit to something that could end up in war. For the most part, American women weren't allowed behind enemy lines in times of war, but congress was discussing it. Max wasn't sure she could shoot another person. The thought of possibly going to war stayed with the young woman in blue while she was in R.O.T.C.

First things first, Max had to get a uniform. After she was measured by the supply sergeant for her blue blouses and slacks, he said, "Would you like me to give you a ride home, if you know what I mean?" The young woman in blue figured the man wanted to have sex with her, even though he was married. She assumed he was married because he was sporting a wedding band on his ring finger. She wondered how many other young women he had propositioned. Max turned the sergeant down. *Welcome to Air Force R.O.T.C.,* she thought to herself. The classes were easy, the marching was light, the officers were nice, but the enlisted were dangerous.

R.O.T.C. was uneventful for a year. The young woman in blue was still not sure about going to war and wasn't sure she wanted to sign on the dotted line. Then one day, the sergeant in charge of records sent a message to Max that he had something for her to sign. He was very friendly to all the cadets and quite popular. The sergeant grabbed her by the collar and pushed her into a closet. He pressed his body against hers. "I can have you anytime I want," he said, before he released the young woman in blue.

Max was afraid of the sergeant. Who would believe her? It was his word against hers. The sergeant was so nice to everybody else. Max was already queasy about signing the line. The sergeant just helped her make up her mind a little earlier. She left R.O.T.C. for good and never looked back.

R.A. IN THE DORM

In the resident advisor interviews, Max was asked what to do in an emergency.

She quickly responded with, "Pull the fire alarm, call the police, get everybody out of the dorm." This answer helped her get chosen by two different dorms to be a resident advisor. She chose to work for Cassie, the kind young woman. Phelps would also be an R.A. in the same dorm, this meant their days as roommates were over. The young woman in blue loved having other young women come to sit on her couch to talk about their problems, just because of her title. But no amount of training made her ready to deal with fights in the middle of the night.

It is three a.m.! Who in god's name is banging the door?. Max rolled out of her upper bunk and slowly opened her door.

"She's going to throw my radio out the window!"

Oh Lord. The young woman in blue dragged herself next door. "What's going on?"

The very neat girl was holding the messy girl's radio out the window. "She's beyond gross. Look at her side of the room!"

Max turned to the messy girl. "You have to admit it is gross."

"Tell her to put down my radio," whined the messy girl.

"Put down her radio."

The very neat girl did as she was told. "I can't live with her anymore."

"I'll get you a room change in the morning. You need to sleep in different places in the meantime. I don't want to be awakened again."

The messy girl went to her boyfriend's to sleep and then moved out of the dorm room in the morning.

Max had earned her pay that quarter.

SPORTS

Tech was going to have a new women's softball team. Tryouts were two weeks long. Cassie was going to them, and Max decided to tag along. Homeruns were not possible with the long fence so the young woman in blue learned to hit the ball where the players were not standing. She learned to slide, but her best feat was catching fly balls in the outfield.

One day the coach had a contest to see who could catch the most balls in a row. Max won. In fact, she did so well the coach finally gave up. The young woman in blue had caught 12 balls in a row and had not dropped a one. But Max was not used to being in the spotlight. In high school she sat on the bench in basketball; she was never first string. The young woman in blue began to panic when she realized she was going to win the prized left field position. So she started dropping balls on purpose until she was told she didn't make the team. Cassie, on the other hand, made the team. She was a solid player that Max watched when she went to the games.

In the fall, the girls' dorms and sororities participated in flag football. Cassie was the quarterback for their dorm team. Max was perfect for center and nose guard because she could knock people down. She loved lining up on the line and having a girl talk smack to her. She would knock the girl down the next play, and that would be the end of the bad words in front of the young woman in blue. One time, a team decided to take Max out of the game. One girl hit her above the knees, and the other hit her below the knees with all their might. The young woman in blue was in shock. In the huddle she whined to Cassie, "Those two girls tried to take me out by hitting above and below my knees."

"Hit them back," said Cassie.

So Max knocked both girls to the ground. As she stood over them she said, "Don't ever do that again." She saw fear in the girls' eyes, so she knew they wouldn't play the trick again. Max loved flag football. She felt so strong, and she liked being so good at something. Because she didn't have to catch the ball she didn't feel pressure to perform like she did in softball.

In November, intramural basketball began. The young woman in blue would not finish the season. She blew out her knee and had knee surgery. It would be a long time until she played sports again.

LEARNING TO KISS

George had dated a lot of women. Max knew that Cassie had dated him. When he asked the young woman in blue out, she said yes because word was that George was a good kisser, but he wouldn't go all the way. This was just what Max was looking for. She felt stupid because of her lack of experience. George probably didn't know that he was giving the young woman in blue kissing lessons. George was as good a kisser as advertised. He was a passionate person, and it came out in his kisses. One time the couple kissed all night. What Max had not planned on was George's falling in love with her. He wanted to take her home to meet his parents in Pennsylvania. The young woman in blue broke it off, and George was very sad. He grabbed her one time and begged her to come back. Max felt nothing in return toward George. It had been just kissing lessons for her.

BIBLE STUDY BUDDY

"I think it's time we quit kidding around and start having a more serious relationship." Ray, age 30, was looking intensely in Max's eyes. Ray was compact. He was short and thin. He had arrived a year earlier to the church where the young woman in blue grew up. She was still attending her childhood Baptist Church, even though she was in college.

"Okay." She had no idea what he had in mind.

"Your mom says you like to study your Bible. I was wondering if you would look at a passage of scripture with me." And that is exactly what they did again and again. It was fun and engaging for the young woman in blue, plus Ray was a sweet guy.

Ray was a Sunday School teacher, and Max started going to his class, even though it was for singles older than college. The study buddies started sitting together in the church services and smiled knowingly at each other when a Bible passage they had studied was mentioned.

Sometimes it felt like Ray could read her mind, and she could read his. They knew when the other was calling on the phone. One day, Ray called her eclectic, and the young woman in blue had to go look it up in the dictionary to figure out what her Bible study buddy had said about her.

They started running into each other outside of church. One time, Ray was on a date at a play that Max was attending with her father.

When Max became a counselor on a Baptist summer camp for girls ages 8-13 Ray wrote to her. But then the writing stopped, and just as she had suspected, he had found someone to marry.

Even though they never dated, in Ray's mind they couldn't continue to be Bible study buddies.

The autumn after summer camp, Sonya, who had raked leaves in high school with the girl in beige and now attended Tech with the young woman in blue, asked Max to come to a small gathering of Sonya's chorus friends. The young woman in blue said she had to study. Then at the last moment, she changed her mind. When they arrived at their destination, it ended up that the host of the gathering was a friend of Ray's. *What a small world*, thought Max, *that Sonya and Ray know the same person*. And then Ray appeared with his big Bible in tow. He locked eyes with the young woman in blue, and ignored Sonya and her chorus friends. "I have one last piece of scripture I want us to look at." Apparently, Ray felt they could come together for one more Bible study before he married.

"How did you know I would be here?"

"I just did."

"But I didn't know I was coming, and I didn't know where I was going."

"I just knew you would be here. Now look at this verse…"

THE BSU PRESIDENT

Cecil Day started the Day's Inn hotel chain. He wanted a Bible in every hotel room, according to his brother Lon. Cecil had died of cancer years before, but his brother continued to tell his story. The young woman in blue listened intently at the Sunday night service at Baptist Church. Lon Day asked if anybody had a testimony he or she would like to share. Max's feet carried her to the front of the church sanctuary because just for a moment she didn't feel shy. She didn't say much. It was her first time to testify in front of her home church. To testify in church means to tell what God is doing in your life. The young woman in blue said she knew Jesus was working in her life as a math major at Tech. Ray got up and walked to the front of the auditorium after Max spoke. He wanted to add an "amen" to the words of the young woman in blue. After the service, Lon Day said he would be speaking at the Tech auditorium in two weeks. "Max, will I be seeing you there?"

"Okay," she said reluctantly because her shy self had returned.

Two weeks later, the young woman in blue dragged herself to a back row of the Tech auditorium. It turned out to be a Baptist Student Union presentation. Max had done many projects with the BSU but didn't consider herself a member.

Lon Day stood up and said before he gave his presentation, "Is Max Burke here?"

Oh, my God! He's calling my name, panicked the young woman in blue. She raised her hand and the whole audience turned around to look at her.

Mr. Day continued, "Well, she is a fine young woman. If you don't already know her, you should get to know her."

Max shrunk in her seat and began to plan her quick exit as soon as the service was over.

As soon as it ended, she began to tip-toe out, looking down at her feet, as usual. She ran into another pair of feet, facing her, with white leather tennis shoes on them. The young woman in blue followed the shoes up a pair of overalls to a cheerful handsome face. "Hi. I'm Mason. I'm the Baptist Student Union president. I already know who you are. Would you like to walk down the hill with me?"

"Uh, okay." How could she resist such a cute man, even if walking to the BSU meant walking in the opposite direction from her dorm?

Mason told jokes.

Max smiled, but she didn't laugh, that is, until they got to the BSU.

The tall cute man told a joke that finally struck a chord with the young woman in blue. She chuckled.

Mason was so pleased that Max had finally laughed that he told the joke again. The young woman in blue laughed again.

"Do you want to eat lunch with me tomorrow?" asked the cute young man.

"Okay."

And they did, the next day and the next.

Only on the third day, Mason had to talk to his girlfriend.

A girlfriend! He has a girlfriend, lamented Max. *What a fool I've been.* And she walked away, hoping to never see Mason again.

CAMP POINT

If she wanted, she could paint the dorms again and make a lot of money the second summer of college. But Max also had an opportunity to be a counselor at a Baptist girls camp called Camp Point in the North Carolina mountains (as mentioned before). She wanted to share with the girls at camp the Bible research she had done with Ray. The only thing was that the pay was small compared to painting the dorms. It was still the summer before Ray got engaged, so the young woman in blue asked Ray what she should do? They were still Bible Study buddies and Ray said he would make up the difference in pay. Max was touched by Ray's gift.

At Camp Point, elementary age girls could swim in the lake, work on crafts, and sing camp songs. The girls in Max's cabin would do a strenuous hike up a mountain and act in silly skits. There were also visiting missionaries from far away lands who told their life stories. The young woman in blue told Bible stories to eager young ears just before bedtime. "Tell us another one, Maxie!" the medium sized girls would say.

"Okay, just one more."

The missionaries the first week were from South America. They showed slides of their home in South America. Their daughter was in the slides. *Oh, my god!* Their daughter was Mason's girlfriend. Max couldn't get away from the BSU president. *Wait a minute. Who's that? That is Ray! Ray is in the pictures.* He worked with the missionaries for a year. Okay, now the young woman in blue knew for sure that God was playing tricks on her. How could her world be so small?

Thankfully, there were new missionaries the next week and Max had no connections to them. She couldn't take many more cosmic jokes anyway. Each week, there were new girls to listen to Max's Bible stories. It felt so good being a storyteller. The summer was a success, even if God played tricks with the young woman in blue the first week.

FRIENDS

It was the fall of her third year at Tech. She liked Hazel, the secretary at the Baptist Student Union, so she decided to see what was new with Hazel. Hazel had a sweet, calming presence that made it easy to be around her. She was always willing to listen to the BSUers that came to sit in her office that overlooked the sitting areas for the students. Max had forgotten about Mason, the cute man, until he came barreling into the secretary's office to announce, "I broke up with my girlfriend."

The young woman in blue shot back, "I don't date."

The cute young man didn't even have to think before he said, "How about we be friends."

Max hesitated and then agreed with an "Okay."

And so they were friends.

"No hugging or touching," said the young woman in blue. "That would be the same as dating."

Mason was a very huggy person, and so Max watched him hug everybody else. But he kept his promise. He did not hug the young woman in blue.

In the eighth month of their friendship, the cute young man asked Max to do the Sunday crossword puzzle with him. This made no sense because the young woman in blue was terrible with words. Her vocabulary was so small she didn't even know the words in the clues. In the BSU building, she sat beside Mason, who promptly put his arm around Max. By this time, she had special feelings for her cute young man, and she thought he was teasing her.

"Hey," the young woman in blue jumped up. "What are you doing? We said no touching."

"I've got to go." Mason ran out the door.

A few minutes later, there was a phone call for Max.

"Hello?"

"It's me," explained Mason.

"Are you going to answer my question now?"

"Yes." He was barely breathing.

"Why did you put your arm around me? Am I just like everybody else? You can touch me without it meaning anything?"

"No. It's just that, well, you are special to me."

"Really?"

"Yes."

"You're special to me, too," Max blurted out.

"Are you teasing me?"

"No. I really mean it."

"What do we do now?" asked Mason.

"Go on a date," answered the young woman in blue.

They went on a date the very next day. It lasted five hours and included talking about making a life together. There were plenty of hugs to make up for the months of not touching. They dated six months before Mason asked Max to marry him. She accepted.

THE CORNFIELD

The summer after Mason and Max went on their first date, they separated for a month. Mason went on choir tour, and Max went to work in a cornfield in South Carolina. She stayed at Aunt June's house and worked with her cousins Jason, Penny, and Sheldon. In the mornings, the cornfield was cold and wet. By noon the sun beat down on their necks, and pollen got stuck in their throats. They were taking part in an experiment. The company was trying out different strands of corn, and the workers were to follow certain procedures to make sure the corn came out right. They popped open one lunch-sized paper bag and put it over the tassel at the top of the plant. They popped another paper bag and put it on the top ear of corn. The scientists, who were in charge, wanted to control what pollinated the plants when they removed the bags. It was a strange and tedious job placing the bags on the plants. Somebody had to stamp a date on all of the bags. The young woman in blue was known for her fast hand. She was removed from her corn duties and put into a shack in the center of the field. She was out of the sun. Boom, boom, boom went the stamp. It sounded like a drum.

Beyond the sound she was making, she could hear her coworkers. A minor league baseball player was stapling frogs in the bags and setting the bags on fire. Those two facts, he was an athlete, and he was a torturer, were the only things she knew about the large man. The young woman in blue was enraged. Although Max rarely spoke up for herself, her emotions came to a boil, and she could not ignore the burning of innocent creatures any longer. Somebody had to save the frogs.

She approached the large man and yelled, "When you can create one frog from nothing, you can torture and kill as many as you like. In the meantime, leave the frogs alone!" Nobody talked to the baseball player like that.

He smiled and said, "All right. I won't burn the frogs anymore."

Max missed Mason terribly. She had never missed anybody like this before. The young woman in blue was supposed to stay for tobacco season, but her heart led her back home to the man that she loved.

BAD GRADES AND KNEE SURGERIES

Max made B's her first quarter at Tech without trying. She had seen the material before. Her second quarter, she had seen some of the material and made all Cs. But her third quarter, she had not seen any of the material before and she had never learned to study or ask for help. She made three Fs and two Ds. She was put on academic probation. The young woman in blue sobbed. She felt helpless against the massive university. How could she be flunking out? Max's parents were so proud of her for being at Tech that she didn't think she could explain the situation to them. She had nowhere to turn but inward. She asked Jesus to help her, and she decided she would learn how to study. The young woman in blue came back strong her first quarter of her sophomore year, back to B's and an A. Life was good.

And then the knee happened. She was in the middle of a basketball game. She pivoted and fell to the ground in pain. Max thought her leg had fallen off, until she opened her eyes and saw nothing. She found out she had torn her anterior cruciate ligament or ACL. Nobody suggested she pull out of college, and it never occurred to the young woman in blue to take off a quarter. She had surgery to remove some torn cartilage and the ligament. No repair was attempted at that time. It was hoped she could get her stability back, with physical therapy. In the meantime, her studies struggled. She failed some courses but was back on track the next quarter. Her knee did not get better. It moved in and out of joint, from side to side. The surgeons suggested a repair. It would be major surgery. Max still did not pull out of college because she did not have any experience with a complicated procedure. The young woman in blue naively believed she could handle a major operation and school. After the surgery, Max was on codeine. She was sitting in fifth quarter calculus and the professor asked for an answer to a problem. The young woman in blue said a forbidden phrase at Tech: "I don't know." She thought she had become dumb, plus the codeine made her not care about mathematics. She walked out of class and never went back. It never occurred to Max to explain her situation or to withdraw because she didn't know how to explain it to herself. She was ashamed of her new stupidity. The young woman in blue didn't know why she was dumb; she just knew she was. She took the F's and said goodbye to Tech. Max left feeling she was a failure.

She brought her grades back up at a community college, before applying to a small college in her hometown of Charlotte. Since she thought she couldn't do math anymore, Max studied religion and philosophy. She also wanted to study religion so that she could argue intelligently with her agnostic father. But most of all, she wanted to study her Bible to learn more about Jesus and get closer to him. Max talked to Jesus more than she talked to people. The mama had taken her children to the local Baptist church since Max was a baby. When the preacher in the pulpit commanded the congregation to bow their heads and pray to Jesus, Max took him seriously. And so she learned to talk to Jesus before she learned to talk to humans at length. Jesus responded by making Max's heart smile. She didn't feel lonely when she told Jesus she loved him. She felt loved back by Jesus' spirit. Max thought if she studied Jesus at college, she would know eternal bliss.

Her knee was another situation. The knee repair did not work, and the young woman in blue was sent to another surgeon named Luanne Marly. Dr. Marly did another ACL repair. The doctor had to be creative because the first repair had used a tendon that could not be used again. With the proper knee brace and physical therapy, the surgery turned out to be a success. Finally Max's knee was fixed. Life was good again.

THE CAR WRECK

After going to other colleges, Caroline, who was the tall thin girl when they were children, and Max ended up at the same small college in Charlotte. The young woman in blue left Tech, and Caroline left her college in Alabama. They both moved back in with their parents, and once again they lived down the street from one another. Since Caroline, whom Max now thought of as the tall young woman, had a new Mustang II, she drove Max to school each day. It was a great time for their relationship. As adults, ages 21, they told each other their dreams, something they hadn't done as children. Caroline dreamed of being a professional golfer. Max hoped to become a Bible professor. The tall young woman still loved to play basketball and therefore started a basketball club at the small college in Charlotte. It was a bonus that she and the young woman in blue could play together for the first time because Max had sat on the bench in high school. It felt so good finally to be together on the same team in a league.

One crisp winter morning, the tall young woman came to pick up the young woman in blue. Caroline held up the rubber padding that had come off her brake pedal.

Max said in a worried voice, "Don't you need to put that back on your car?"

"Naw, I'll do it later. We've got to get you to class so you can present your philosophy report."

"Are you sure?" The young woman in blue was concerned.

"Forget it." And the tall young woman tossed the rubber cover into the back seat.

On their way to school, they talked about their next basketball game and how much fun it was to be together on the court. As she dropped off Max, Caroline said, "It's going to be a great day!" Her positive attitude was contagious. Since she didn't have a class for another hour, Caroline decided to drive down the street to get a soda and candy. The young woman in blue waved goodbye.

After class, Max decided to track down the tall young woman to tell her how her philosophy project had gone. She couldn't find her anywhere, so the young woman in blue asked one of Caroline's professors if she had seen the tall young woman.

The professor said in a strange voice. "Caroline didn't come to school today."

Hmm?

So Max called Caroline's home. Her brother Stuart answered the phone. The young woman in blue could hear Caroline's family screaming.

"Where is Caroline?" demanded Max.

Between sobs, Stuart said, "Caroline's dead. She was in a car wreck this morning."

The young woman in blue dropped the receiver and ran back to the professor.

"They said Caroline's dead!"

"Then it's confirmed. All we knew was she was in critical condition."

The professor called Mason, and Mason came and got Max to take her home.

Max walked down the street to Caroline's home. The house was already filled with family and friends. Even Ms. Boston, the high school basketball coach, and Ms. Leadman, the high school A.P. English teacher, were there.

The young woman in blue blurted out in anger to Ms. Boston, "She always dreamed you would visit her at her home, and it takes her dying for you to show up."

Ms. Boston looked at Max with pity and great sadness in her eyes.

Somebody said, "There was no brake action. She slid under a tractor trailer truck."

The young woman in blue told everybody about the rubber cover that came off the brake that morning.

At the funeral there was an open casket. Caroline looked like she was faking. Max leaned over the body and whispered, "Come on. Get up. I'll tell everybody to get out of the room if you'll just get up."

But the tall young woman didn't get up.

On Friday, Max was asked at the last minute to say something on behalf of Caroline in the small college's weekly chapel service.

All that quiet from all those years added up in her heart. The young woman in blue stood tall and spoke clearly about her childhood friend. She told the story of just the week before, when Caroline had said she was going to live to a ripe old age. Max had said she would die young in a blaze of glory. But as it turned out, Caroline had been the one to die young. The life of the young woman in blue had been spared. She had not been in the car when it wrecked. Jesus must want her to live a long life. Caroline's life and her life had crossed destinies.

Afterwards, she tried to get away from the crowd. The dean of the college grabbed Max's arm and said, "That was an awesome sermon."

"I know," admitted the young woman in blue.

But no breakthrough in speaking could replace the big hole in her heart, a hole that would never leave.

Soon after Caroline's death, the tall young woman began to visit Max in nighttime dreams. Caroline said the young woman in blue was the only one who could see her. She missed her life on earth, and she enjoyed visiting Max. The young woman in blue would awake in the middle of the night with a dream fresh in her head. It felt like Caroline had really been there. Max was spooked by the dreams, but she never told anybody about them. At first, the dreams came every night. Eventually, they came less often. Ten years after Caroline's death, Max still dreamed of her friend about once a month. The dreams no longer spooked her because they had become a part of her normal.

VIRGINS AND BLUE JEANS

The little girl in red grew up and wanted to share her whole self with the man she loved, body and soul. MM took longer than most people to mature. She was twenty-one. Now, the young woman in blue wanted to make love.

Mason and Max were both virgins before they married. Mason was a conservative Christian who did not believe in sex before marriage. The young woman in blue was more liberal. She thought as long as two people were in love, they didn't have to be married to make love. But she didn't want to take a chance on becoming pregnant before she married. She feared being shamed by her mother and by her peers.

Max was in love with Mason. He was good looking, smart, and spiritual. Mason had memorized a large portion of the Book of Romans in the New Testament and the young woman in blue was fascinated by this feat. She couldn't even memorize the short chemistry formulas for her tests, let alone a few Bible verses. Mason was a genius in an area in which Max fell behind.

Mason was also in love with Max. In particular, he loved that she was on a quest to discover Jesus in prayer, in worship, and in scripture. Mason thought the young woman in blue was quite spiritual. He also found her attractive physically and consequently wanted to move up the wedding date so they could finally make love.

Max also wanted to move up the wedding date. She had to admit she wanted to have sex sooner than later. The young woman in blue also felt the world was unsafe when Caroline died. She wanted to rest from danger in Mason's loving arms. Her fantasy was that her future husband could save her from pain.

Mason and Max married five months after Caroline died. Finally they were able to enjoy making love. A Christian book introduced them to the basics of sex. Mason and the young woman in blue had a happy sex life for many years. But most of all, they were best friends.

Max had a problem with initial touch. When someone first touched her on her skin, it felt like she was being pinched or burned. But after the initial touch, her nervous system calmed down. Her lips, the hair on her head, and her hands were not hypersensitive like the rest of her body. So if the initial touch was a kiss on the lips, then she had no problem. She was able to progress into sex like anybody else. But if Mason first put his arm around Max, she sometimes pulled away. Things went better if the young woman in blue made the first move, because her hands were not extra sensitive to touch. It was only the first touch from another that bothered Max. Mason and the young woman in blue did not understand at the time why Max pulled away when Mason tried to give her a hug in the middle of the day. It would be many years later before an explanation would show itself.

In their first year of marriage, Mason gave Max her first pair of blue jeans for her birthday. She absolutely loved those jeans and wore them almost every day. Max was so thankful for a husband who knew what made her happy. In those jeans, she continued to be the young woman in blue.

PHILOSOPHY CLASS

Derek Hamilton was like no other professor. For one reason, he insisted on being called by his first name, instead of Dr. Hamilton. The young woman in blue took a required philosophy class from him at the small college in Charlotte. She had no idea what the word "philosophy" meant; she just knew she had to take the course. The first day of class, Derek said he wanted the students to choose to argue, "Is it better to give or is it better to receive?" Max knew everybody would choose "to give," so she chose "to receive." First, who would be receiving all those gifts? Plus, humility was needed to receive. Humility was a virtue. On and on went her proof. The philosophy professor was impressed.

After class, the young woman in blue said to Derek, "I don't know what philosophy is."

The professor replied, "Do any of us?"

They studied Plato's *Symposium on Love* in class. The young woman's eyes glowed. She had found her niche. She went on to study more Plato, Aristotle, Søren Kierkegaard, and Thomas Aquinas. She felt akin to Kierkegaard, hiding out in his sister's house and only going out for his daily walk.

Derek liked to have parties with wine and classical music and good conversation. Near Max's graduation, he announced, "Max is the best Christtian philosophy student I have ever had."

Before she married, Derek told the young woman's mother that he wished she wouldn't marry. He wished she would go to Princeton instead and become a philosophy Ph.D. student. But Max got married and went to seminary as a M.Div. student.

On the first day of seminary, Max ran into Derek. She had no idea what Derek was doing on the campus. She would never see him there again. "Remember you are the smartest person here." He told the young woman in blue. It was good to hear because seminary, unlike philosophy, would be a challenge.

GRADUATION PARTY

Lila, aka My Baby, graduated from high school the same quarter Max finally graduated from college. The mama threw a backyard barbeque party. The mother-in-law of the young woman in blue had sewn Max a beautiful yellow dress. Most of the young woman in blue's time was spent talking and dancing with Derek Hamilton. She saw a tall figure slip into the backyard. She couldn't believe her eyes. It was Coach Rizzo, aka the man who hid behind the magazine.

"What are you doing here?" Max asked a little too bluntly.

"I came to see you," the coach answered honestly. "How are you doing?"

"Good." The young woman in blue sat down next to Coach Rizzo. She felt a surge of joy.

They didn't say much more. Their relationship had always been one of few words.

Mason found them together and filled the empty space with the words. The young woman in blue was a bit embarrassed by Mason's words. They seemed a bit out of place, for he was rambling on about this and that. Why did Mason have to talk so much? Didn't he understand that a lot of words weren't needed.

The young woman in blue and the man who hid behind the magazine didn't use anymore words after Mason left them alone. Still, she was so excited that her favorite high school teacher had come to see her.

BABIES

Max and Mason had been advised by one of the ministers at their church to enjoy a full year of marriage before trying to have children. As soon as that year was up, the young woman in blue wanted a baby. She didn't know why she wanted children so much. Perhaps she wanted to create people like herself. Or maybe it was hormones that egged her on. All she knew was she wanted babies. It took a few months to get pregnant. It was exciting to think about the future with a new baby, but it was yucky to be sick every day of the first trimester.

The second trimester was baby showers and shopping to get ready for the couple's first born. The third trimester, Max just wanted the baby out. Her water broke about three a.m., two weeks before the due date. The labor pains came slowly, so the young woman in blue sent her husband to work. By the afternoon, the doctor said Max needed to come over to the hospital. The labor moved too slowly, so the young woman in blue was given Pitocin. The drug made the contractions very intense and hurt a great deal. Max began to cry that she wanted to go home. She finally got an epidural, which calmed her down. It wasn't until the delivery that the doctor found out why the labor had moved so slowly. The baby was strangled with the umbilical cord around his neck four times. He didn't breathe immediately.

"Come on baby!" urged the doctor, as he shook little Zebulon. Mason prayed. The young woman in blue was very frightened. After what felt like forever, baby Zeb sighed his first breath. He didn't cry. Zeb had a head full of jet black hair and was beautiful to look at.

When Max got newborn Zeb to herself, she said to him, "You just came from seeing Jesus, didn't you?'

Zeb gurgled and gave a half smile.

"I knew it!" declared the young woman in blue. Emotionally, it felt odd that this newly-created person was not a rental. Max kept expecting the hospital to call and ask for its baby back. How could their home be his home now?

Zeb was an easy baby. He loved being around Mason and Max. He cooed and jumped in his jumping contraption that hung in the doorway. Zeb smiled and laughed with everybody who paid attention to him. But Max wasn't ready for all the attention Zeb gave her. She had never been watched so constantly. Also, Zeb wanted to be held beyond the young woman in blue's comfort zone. Max almost always put Zeb's needs and desire before her own. Having a baby was exhausting physically and emotionally. Fortunately, Zeb took a lot of naps, and the young woman in blue slept, too.

Nine months later, the young woman in blue said she was ready for another baby. She thought Zeb could use a playmate. Max became pregnant that very night! That was quite a shock. Her pregnancy was just like her first. Her water broke in the early morning hours again, and she went to the hospital in the afternoon. This time the labor progressed normally. Baby Sarah was healthy and screamed to let everyone know she had arrived. She was pretty and had a full head of dark brown hair. Sarah was not content with her family in their apartment. She wanted out and would fuss until she got outside. The young woman in blue would place the baby in a milk crate in a red wagon. Zeb would hop in the front of the wagon, and off to the zoo they would go for hours. Sarah was a very busy baby. She rifled through everything she could get her hands on. When Zeb went to the nursery at church, he liked to visit with the workers. He would coo and chuckle with them. Sarah had no part of the workers. She was busy pulling toys off the shelf. Sarah would shake each toy and then toss it to the ground. When Max picked up Zeb from the nursery, he clung to her and acted like she had been gone for years. Sarah, on the other hand, was occupied and barely took notice of her mother. Zeb and Sarah were as different as night and day. Max loved them both very much.

One parenting book that belonged to the young woman in blue said that toddlers explore their environment a little at a time. They wander about and then return to a parent, to touch in physically and emotionally. Zeb was textbook. He touched in with Max and Mason all day. But Sarah, like her mother when she was a toddler, did not touch in. She pulled away from her parents and stayed away from them all day. At night, she awoke screaming.

Watching her daughter reminded the young woman in blue of her years of loneliness as a child. It was as if history were repeating itself. Max felt great pain in her heart for Sarah and for little Max.

The young woman in blue thought that if Sarah would not touch in with her, then she would touch in with Sarah, when her daughter was too tired to pull away. So every night at Sarah's bedtime, Max climbed in the bed with Sarah. She rubbed her daughter's back and told her she loved her. After a few months of this, Sarah began to be a huggy child. She began to touch in during the daytime, and she had fewer times of screaming in her sleep. To this day, Sarah comes and gets her hugs from her mother and father. She is much more adjusted to touch than Max. Even though hugs are difficult for Max, she knows they are a way Sarah conveys her love. So Max receives them and gives them with much love in her heart.

THE PROBLEM TREE

Faith lived a few blocks from Mason and the young woman in blue. Faith liked to pray, not just little prayers, but half an hour and longer prayers. Each time they met, Faith asked Max about her life, and then Faith told the young woman in blue about her own joys and problems. Next, Faith prayed, and Max listened. The young woman in blue added a short prayer. She had never met someone like Faith, who believed so whole heartedly that prayer worked.

Mason and Max bought a piece of property on which they hoped to build a house. It was a few blocks from Faith's house and Mason's and Max's apartment. The property had a half-dead tree that posed a problem to future construction. The giant tree sat at the top of the hill next to the street and could fall at any time because it was half dead. If it were to fall, it could knock over any of the neighbors' fences that surrounded the property. The tree would need to go, but it would be expensive. The young couple did not have the money to chop down the tree because they were living on a budget that did not allow for tree removal.

Faith suggested that she and Max pray over the problem tree. The young woman in blue felt silly putting her hand on the tree, while asking Jesus to help with the situation. But Faith insisted. They prayed over the tree every chance they got for a month, until Mason and Max moved out of the neighborhood.

A year later, the couple had forgotten all about the tree. They had given up on fixing the tree problem, due to continued lack of finances. They no longer lived in the same neighborhood as the tree, therefore it was no longer something they saw every day. One morning, a friend from the old neighborhood called, saying they had no electricity because of Mason and Max's tree.

"What are you talking about?" asked Mason.

The friend said the tree had fallen in the street and knocked out the power lines. Since it had fallen in the street, the city had already begun to cut up the tree. No fences had been knocked down.

There was no way to prove that prayer was the reason behind the tree falling perfectly in the street, so that no fences were taken out and only power lines were knocked down. Plus Max and Mason didn't have to pay to get the tree cut down and cut up. Nonetheless, Max called Faith and laughed at the way things worked out. Faith sent up a prayer and rejoiced in her Lord.

THE CALLING

Max missed school. She absolutely loved learning about Jesus. She enjoyed reading scripture very much. The young woman in blue helped to teach a Bible study in a government housing project. She and Mason also conducted an adult Sunday school class at their church.

Max told her husband that she wanted to go to seminary, but Mason replied honestly that he didn't want his wife to have more schooling than he had. It was a tough blow to the young woman in blue.

One day when the children were taking their nap, Max fell on her face and begged Jesus to let her go to seminary. Since Mason didn't want to be left behind, she prayed that he could go, too. As the young woman in blue poured out her heart, she saw what looked like a mist fill the room. The mist felt very holy. Max was not shocked or astounded by the mist. She felt loved, surrounded by it.

A few minutes later, Mason came home for lunch. He immediately fell to the floor because the mist demanded it. "What have you been praying?" Mason cried barely lifting his head from the floor.

"I asked for us to go to seminary. It feels like Jesus is saying that it was his idea to begin with and that he is calling us to seminary. He is waiting for an answer. I didn't want to answer without you."

"Just tell him we'll go," croaked Mason.

Max told Jesus that she and Mason would go to seminary. The mist went away immediately, and the couple could stand again.

The young woman in blue didn't tell anyone else about the mist, and she and Mason never mentioned it again. Max didn't feel like other people would understand something that she herself could barely describe. There was a lot about her world she didn't feel translated to the regular world.

ANOTHER CAR WRECK

The young woman in blue felt in her gut a prompting to pray over everybody in the house. The children, ages five months and almost two, were already asleep. Max put her hands on each child's head and prayed for protection. Then she prayed for Mason and herself.

The next morning the young woman in blue dropped Sarah off at the mama's house. Sarah did not enjoy long trips. That is why she was going to spend a day at her grandmother's house while Max and Zeb went on a 90-minute trip to a big town in North Carolina. The young woman in blue and Zeb were going on a social visit with Lila, also known as My Baby. The car, an economy-size Dodge Colt, was only a few months old. Zeb's car seat was brand new. Air bags were only installed in luxury cars in the 1980s, and there was no law saying car seats should be in the back seat. This meant Zeb's car seat was in the front on the passenger's side of the car. Zeb was delighted to talk to his mother the whole way. The almost two-year-old loved Hot Wheels and Matchbox cars, miniature toy cars. He had a big collection in the rear of the car. He chirped on about his cars, happy to have Max's attention all to himself.

They were almost all the way to the big town when the car slipped off the edge of the pavement on the passenger's side of the car. The young woman in blue over-corrected the car so that they were headed over the yellow divider line in the middle of the highway. When Max put her foot on the brake pedal, there was no brake action. The car raced across the oncoming lane and hit a concrete pillar on the side of the road. The pillar was on the property of a Trucking Company. It was a bright yellow, thick pole, used to mark the driveway entrance. The pillar pushed over to a diagonal slant from the impact of the car. It became a ramp, and the car shot up the concrete pole. The Dodge Colt was airborne until the front tires hit the top of a truck cab. The car slid down until the bumpers locked up. Then all was quiet.

In those few seconds it took to wreck, the young woman in blue saw Jesus with his arms stretched out ready to catch her and Zeb. The car hung in the air, and Max said calmly to her son, "We've had a wreck."

Zeb began to cry, "Oh, Mama! We aren't supposed to wreck."

Truckers peeked into the window of the Colt, afraid of what they would see. Except for whiplash, Zeb was unharmed. Max also had whiplash and was bleeding on her arm from the broken window. Zeb began to scream that he wanted out of his car seat. The young woman in blue released Zeb, and he crawled over her into one of the trucker's arms. The secretary of the company came out of the trucking office when she heard the wreck. She sidled up to Max and asked who she should call. Max's brain was in a fog, but she finally said, "Mason." Mason was called, and then the ambulance arrived.

The young woman in blue was strapped to a backboard, and Zeb climbed into a paramedic's arms. "My cars, Mama, my cars!" wailed Zeb.

"Your father will get them," promised Max.

Lila met them at the hospital and took Zeb away with her. The young woman in blue was x-rayed, probed, and then released. Eventually, Mason, the mama, and Sarah arrived. Sarah was not a huggy child yet, but she clung to her mother and did not let go. She seemed to understand that she almost lost her mama. They all went to see the Colt. It was crushed in every part of the car except where Max and Zeb had been sitting. The young woman in blue fell to the ground and wept. She and her son were lucky to be alive. Her whiplash from the wreck was very painful for a long time. Every time Max sees the chiropractor these days, she is reminded of the day the brakes failed and she saw Jesus with his arms out wide.

THE FREE HOUSE

One morning, the young woman in blue prayed a selfish prayer. She prayed for a house. Max and Mason had spent their money on seminary and didn't have money for a house. So it was kind of selfish to wish for both school and a house. Max prayed like never before. She asked Jesus to show her how to get a house. Lilly came to mind. She was the inner-city Baptist missionary who owned two houses that Max and Mason knew about. The more the young woman in blue prayed, the more she felt she should ask Lilly for a house. Her logical side told her that was ridiculous to get a house for free. People didn't just ask for houses and expect to get them. Finally, in late afternoon of the same day, Max went to see Lilly. Now Lilly was a person bathed in prayer. She was the one who had taught Faith to pray. Lilly had a direct pipeline to God. She prayed for money, and then she would find cash in her mailbox or at her doorstep. Lilly served God 24/7. She was a lifeline to the poorest of the poor. They came to her door anytime, day or night. Lilly was always willing to serve.

Max had been working with the poor for a few years. When her fellow seminary students were afraid of the homeless men at the community kitchen to which they were assigned, the young woman in blue was eating and talking with the kitchen's guests. She felt no fear of the homeless, just an overpowering love for each individual. But unlike Lilly, who seemed to give and give, Max was running out of fuel. She was burning out.

The young woman in blue knocked on Lilly's front door. The elder woman opened the door and said, "It's about time you got here. I've been waiting all day for you."

Max stuttered, "I'm-I'm supposed to ask about buying a house from you."

"Buy? I'm supposed to *give* you a house. Most people don't know it, but I own a lot of houses in this neighborhood. I'm thinking you would do well in the one north of the zoo."

The young woman in blue was flabbergasted and a bit spooked. In that moment, Max realized nothing was really free. She knew Lilly expected her to keep working with the poor. Mason also wanted Max to continue to work with the poor, plus their church wanted to pay the couple for their work in the inner city. But the young woman in blue was tired. She would not accept the house and the expected life of a full time inner city minister. Little by little Max dropped out of her work with the poor.

SARAH DRIVES THE CAR

Zeb had a fleet of toy Tonka trucks to play with in the sand and dirt. Mason was helping a neighbor build his house a few blocks away. The young woman in blue loaded up the toy trucks and tossed the two children in the front seat of the giant, old Lincoln Continental. After all, it was only a few blocks; who needed to buckle up? Max started the car and heard a crunch. She had driven over something with the back passenger side tire. She put the car in park and went to inspect the damage. The young woman in blue looked under the Continental. She saw one of Zeb's Tonka trucks crushed beside the tire. Max, on her hands and knees, pulled the truck out from behind the wheel. The tire began to move.

What? What is happening? thought the young woman in blue. Max stood up and saw toddler Sarah standing up in the driver's seat, holding the steering wheel. The car kept moving. It was headed for the street. The first thing the young woman in blue thought of was the people who found super human strength and lifted a car off the ground. Surely she could stop the Lincoln. Max ran to the front of the car and stared Sarah in the eye. Sarah was laughing with joy. She was driving the car! No amount of pushing stopped the car. The young woman in blue had to think quickly. She ran to the driver's door and threw it open. The car was in the street and heading for the fire hydrant in the neighbor's yard. Max tried to jump in the car, but the Lincoln Continental lept forward. She would have to figure in the movement of the car. The young woman in blue finally understood the speed of the car and jumped in the driver's seat, knocking over Sarah. She jammed on the brake. The car was pushed onto the hydrant.

Zeb exclaimed, "Why did Sarah get to drive the car?"

Max blurted out, "Sarah did not have permission to drive the car. She just did it anyway."

The young woman in blue did not want her neighbor to find her car in the middle of their yard. She backed off the hydrant and drove the few blocks to the building site. Max fell into her husband's arms while Zeb chattered, "Mama ran over my truck, and Sarah drove the car."

"What?" asked Mason.

"It's all true," said the young woman in blue.

"Maybe you should tell me the whole story."

Max poured out the whole tale, and they all marveled that no one had gotten hurt.

PROFESSOR DONALDSON

Grayson Donaldson was Max's academic advisor at seminary. She taught New Testament and Preaching. Woman preachers were forbidden in the Baptist church of the young woman in blue. So she was pretty sure she would not take preaching class. It wouldn't look good on her record if she wanted to get a job in her denomination. Max saw Dr. Donaldson once a week in Supervised Ministry class. SM1 was where first year students reported on their assigned ministry. Grayson Donaldson's advisees worked at a community kitchen four hours a week. The young woman in blue did great at the community kitchen because she had previous years of experience working with the poor. She had helped lead a Bible study in a government housing project for three years and had been a part of a weekly meal for the poor in her neighborhood with Lilly and Faith for another two years.

She did not do so great at reporting in to her peers and advisor. Max took every response to her reports as hurtful criticism. One day, a remark hurt so bad that Dr. Donaldson recommended that the young woman in blue contact a therapist who was putting together a group for adult children of alcoholics. Grayson Donaldson said she herself was an adult child of an alcoholic, and she knew what it felt like to be hypersensitive to what others said. Max could tell Dr. Donaldson cared, but she really didn't want to be in a group that had anything to do with her drunk father. She ended up calling the therapist anyway because she was tired of feeling so terrible from others' comments. The therapy group fell through, but the therapist recommended that the young woman in blue start individual therapy. Individual therapy showed the young woman in blue that she had critical parents and that she expected to be picked on. Her father was especially critical and unpredictable because he was an alcoholic. Her mother was just critical. Therapy became a wonderful, safe place with kind words from a kind person. Max realized that she hated herself and was ashamed of her childhood. It would take years of therapy to counteract the self-hatred. In the meantime, therapy helped immediately, with supervised ministry. Little by little, the young woman in blue didn't take comments so personally. The more she learned not to pick on herself, the more she didn't see the world as picking on her.

The Methodist women ministers were preaching at their churches. After hearing the women preachers in the seminary chapel services, Max decided she wanted to preach.

Grayson Donaldson edited Max's first sermon. She invited her student to her house and went over the details of the sermon. The young woman in blue would be preaching at a Baptist church that had invited Mason to preach. Mason suggested to their minister that Max preach instead. Mason knew that many Baptists weren't quite sure what to do with women preachers, so he wanted to get his wife as many opportunities as possible. The young woman in blue was received very well in the pulpit. She preached about Zacchaeus who had climbed a tree to see Jesus. By the end of the sermon, Max suggested the church throw open the doors and climb trees. She got many compliments on her sermon.

Back at school, Dr. Donaldson said, "Watching you change was one of the best parts of my year." Max ended up taking five classes from Grayson Donaldson; three of them were preaching classes.

SEMINARY AND THERAPY

Seminary changed Max and Mason. Mason threw himself into his studies. He had little time for the young woman in blue and the children. Mason said he would finish seminary as quickly as possible, and afterwards he would engage in home life again. This did not sit well with Max. It meant she took care of the children most of the time and did most of the cleaning. When the young woman in blue challenged her husband on his behavior, he got angry and refused to negotiate any middle ground.

Max changed, too. She wanted equality in her marriage for the first time. Not only was she doing the bulk of the work, she had been trained at a Southern Baptist workshop to leave the major decisions to her husband. She could lend advice, but in the end, he decided for them the most important decisions in their lives. Mason agreed with this ethic. Max was beginning to disagree. She had also put Mason's needs before her own needs as much as possible. The young woman in blue had always thought it was selfish to ask for anything. But now, she was beginning to think that having a self was not selfish after all.

The young woman in blue had gone to psychotherapy when Grayson Donaldson had suggested it. Her therapist, Sheila, was a kind soul who listened to Max like she had rarely been listened to before. The young woman in blue felt safe and private in therapy. She rarely looked Sheila in the eye. It would take years and another therapist before she could keep a steady gaze. For the first time in her life, Max talked about Sally, who ran through the airplane propeller and how that had changed her life. The young woman in blue found it a relief to give her burdens to Sheila. She was also learning just a little bit how to love herself, or at least not to hate herself so much.

Max's confidence grew, and she confronted Mason. They fought and Mason said he was leaving. The young woman in blue thought he meant permanently, so she stood in the door to block the exit. Mason shoved Max. The young woman in blue retaliated by punching her husband in the jaw. Mason became so mad that he threw Max across the kitchen. As she lay crumpled on the floor, the young woman in blue felt very frightened because she realized that Mason was stronger than she.

Mason leaned down and said in a low voice, "Don't you ever touch me again." Then he walked out of the house.

Max was afraid to stay with her husband, but she was also afraid to go. When Mason returned many hours later, the young woman in blue said they had to go to therapy to talk about what had happened.

The husband and wife went to couples' therapy. Mason said everything was in Max's imagination. When they left therapy, Mason said, "Don't you ever tell another soul about this again." This made the young woman in blue even more afraid of her husband, but she did not leave yet.

SHE'S HIDING UNDER THE TABLE: ONE WOMAN'S LIFE WITH ASPERGER'S AND DEPRESSION

PART FIVE – THE WOMAN IN RED

WOMAN IN RED IS BORN

July 1989, Age 27: The young woman in blue signed up for Liberation Theologies. It was a month long summer class that met three hours every week night. Max had never met the professor, Roberta Punch. Dr. Punch said she wasn't going to teach the class after the first week; the students would. Since liberation movements (feminist, African-American, and Latin American) happened in community, the students would be put in groups of three or four to work together on their projects. The young woman in blue dreaded working in a group. She preferred to work alone. Her two partners in her group were only interested in themselves. They didn't particularly like Max. The young woman in blue hated the childhood loneliness that was generated in her by working with the narcissistic project partners. Despite their differences, the three students produced a creative, fun project, which included class participation. In fact, all the projects had the entire class participating. It was very therapeutic.

In the middle of the month, the young woman in blue flew to New York City with Cassie, the kind young woman from her college days. Max had always wanted to visit NYC since her father had worked on a computer project there when Maxie was young. Since that time, the daddy absolutely glowed when he spoke of New York.

Mostly, the young woman in blue and Cassie walked the busy streets of Manhattan. They saw the Empire State Building and took a cab to Wall Street. Cassie wanted to see the Statue of Liberty. Max didn't see any reason to go, but she didn't tell Cassie that. She went anyway. The young woman in blue was pretty sure everybody on the ferry over to the statue was Japanese except herself and Cassie. She couldn't understand a word being said. Then she heard a woman's voice in English. Max looked at Cassie, but Cassie wasn't speaking.

"Over here," said the Statue of Liberty. The ferry was right in front of the statue's face.

Huh? thought the young woman in blue.

The statue continued, "Listen up. Free yourself before you free other women."

What? Max thought to the statue.

"You heard me. Free yourself before you free other women."

Then the ferry was past the statue's face.

Later that day, the two women watched the movie *Working Girl*. In it, Carly Simon sings the song "Let the River Run." The second line of the chorus is "Let all the dreamers wake the nation." It became the favorite song of the young woman in blue.

After she got home, Max told Roberta Punch about the Statue of Liberty. "What do you think she meant?" asked the young woman in blue.

Professor Punch responded, "If she told you that, she must think you are smart enough to figure it out."

Liberation Theologies class was so moving that Max felt a love for everybody in the class, including her project partners. It didn't mean she liked their personalities any more than before, but she felt a closeness to all her classmates because of their shared experience. Roberta Punch was so touched by the spirit of the class that she gave everybody an A.

The marriage of the young woman in blue had become violent emotionally and a little physically. Eventually, she would free herself and become the woman in red because red was still her favorite color, after all these years.

BACKPACKING

December 1989, Age 28: Fall semester began, and Max was already running behind. She had missed the first colloquy group for the large required Psychology and Religion class. In the small colloquy, the students were supposed to discuss the required readings and write papers. The woman in red looked up the colloquy leader's name, Macy Umber. She was teaching two other colloquies that had not met yet. *Oh, good, I'll go to one of those and make up for the missed class*, thought Max.

Macy was a redheaded doctoral student. She held the door open to the classroom. She was a handsome woman. Macy's eyes sparkled at the woman in red.

At lunchtime, Macy would sit on the chapel steps, like many other students. Max would sidle up to her and talk about Zeb and Sarah. Macy would cover a range of subjects. Max thought, *She is a good looking nerd, and I am attracted to her.* The two women soon became friends.

In December, when the semester came to an end, Macy said she would love to go backpacking with the woman in red anytime. Max had knee surgery in a few weeks and needed to clear her head. She asked the nerdy woman if she would be willing to go camping in winter. Macy loved backpacking so much, she would go any time, even in the cold.

It was snowing the evening they arrived in the North Carolina Mountains. The women didn't walk too far that night because it was already dark. After they were in the tent, Macy read the *Tao of Pooh* out loud. She asked what the woman in red thought about what she had read. Max had been a philosophy major, so she had plenty to discuss. This pleased the nerdy woman.

The next morning, the women backpacked further into the wilderness. They had to walk through many streams. The women had to take off their boots and socks to walk barefoot through the chilly water. Macy had a hand towel to dry their feet.

When they set up camp, the woman in red asked the nerdy woman, "Do you date men or women?"

Macy was not out at school, so she answered, "Yes."

Max chuckled at the nerdy woman's cleverness and then said, "I am attracted to both sexes." What she really wanted to say was, "I am attracted to you." But she didn't.

The women left their backpacks at camp and went on a vigorous hike that took all their attention. They rested against some large boulders. The giant rock the woman in red was pressed against whispered in her ear, "I am here for you. You are a beautiful person."

Who are you? thought Max to the rock.

The voice in the rock said, "I am the female spirit. I am here to help you explore the divine feminine in the world."

What about Jesus? thought the woman in red.

"I'm here, and I want you to get to know the female spirit."

Okay, I'll have to think about all of this.

Max turned to the nerdy woman. "The rock just talked to me."

Macy asked, "What did she say?"

"How did you know it was a she?" responded the woman in red.

"I just know some things" the nerdy woman smiled.

When they arrived back at the campsite, Macy announced, "I'm not looking for a relationship. I wish I could have a weekend lover."

"Oh," was all the woman in red could think to say.

As they backpacked out of the wilderness to go home, Max blurted out, "I wouldn't mind being your weekend lover."

The nerdy woman pretended like she didn't hear.

They drove back to Charlotte, and the spell was broken. The woman in red thought, *What was wrong with me in the wilderness? I must have sounded like I was crazy.*

But for the next few days, Max could not get Macy off her mind. She decided to go talk to the nerdy woman the night before her knee surgery. When the woman in red was in Macy's attic, she felt shy all of a sudden. Finally, she confessed that she really liked the nerdy woman.

Macy pulled out a sheet of paper with writing on it and read aloud all the reasons she should not be in relationship with Max. "Number one: You are married. I was in a relationship with a married woman for seven years. I swore I wouldn't ever do that again. Number two: You haven't turned thirty yet. I was just in a relationship with a younger woman, and I want someone closer to my age. Number three: If you get a divorce, your husband is going to blame me for your break up. I do not want to break up a marriage. Number four: We are both students and barely have enough money to support ourselves. We won't be well off."

The woman in red laughed. "You like me too!"

"Yes," confessed the nerdy woman.

"That's all I needed to know before surgery," Max announced and left Macy alone in her attic.

Within a week, the woman in red knew she was in love. She was sorry she had not left Mason before. Max said to her husband, "I'm leaving. I'm in love with Macy." Mason didn't say anything. He rocked back and forth in his rocking chair and glared at the woman in red. Max was very scared of that glare. She didn't know what Mason would do. She moved out that very day. She took the children with her to her father's house.

LEAVING HOME

December 1989, Age 28: Max stood on her crutches with a child on either side of her. It was freezing and she was begging the daddy to let her in.

"Not until you apologize for what you said to me." He stood between the door and the woman in red.

Two months before, she had said his drinking hurt her. It was the first and last time she ever confronted her father. Max swallowed her pride and said, "I'm sorry for what I said." She wasn't really sorry. The woman in red was cold and afraid of her husband. She needed a place to stay. The mama's husband and the mama wouldn't have her. So that left the daddy.

Her father smiled, "Come on in. Get out of the cold."

Max hobbled into Grandma Maxine's old bedroom. Her grandmother had died the month before. It was late, and the children fell right to sleep. The woman in red trembled because she didn't feel safe. What if Mason came and dragged her back home? He was so mad when she left.

Max cried to Jesus. After fifteen minutes, she saw a figure at the end of the bed. It said, "You are safe now. Go to sleep."

Maybe it's an angel, thought the woman in red, as calmness came over her, and she fell asleep.

Mason would appear the next morning. The daddy would turn him away. Max had left her husband, and she would never go back.

DR. SAUL

Winter/Spring 1990, Age 28: Ronald Saul was one of the professors of the required theology class at the seminary. He was also the father of Emma Saul from the famed singing duo, the Artic Women. Max's children were big Artic Women fans. So was Macy. The woman in red was yet to be a fan. Eventually, she would come around. In the meantime, she had a hard time following Dr. Saul in class. Her mind was on her divorce and the lesbian relationship she was beginning.

A big part of theology class was the theology paper each student was required to write. Max titled her paper "When Jesus Was a Girl." When she was eight, the little girl in red invited Jesus into her heart. She didn't turn into a boy, so Jesus must have turned into a girl when he was living in Max's heart. The paper of the woman in red was about her experience with the church, especially since she had fallen in love with Macy. Mostly, she was not accepted in the Baptist church anymore. She had felt at home there for so many years.

It was also about her dilemma, in that a part of her wanted to listen to the more radical feminist lesbians who no longer worshiped a male deity. Jesus wasn't really a girl. He had lived life as a man and was also a male part of the trinity of God. There was a part of Max that needed space away from men. She didn't write about the female spirit in her paper, but she discussed her with Macy.

Ronald Saul read the paper and asked Max to lunch. The woman in red's fear of Mason had expanded to all men. She explained this to Dr. Saul, and he seemed to understand. This did not stop him from discussing Artic Women sightings with the woman in red after class. Dr. Saul also stopped and talked to Zeb and Sarah when he saw them. He even got them a signed tape cassette cover from Emma.

Years later, another of Ronald Saul' daughters died. Max went to the memorial service and gave some of her writing to her professor. She wanted to give Dr. Saul a part of herself. A few weeks later, she saw Emma at a restaurant. The woman in red introduced herself and asked Emma to say hello to her father. Emma said, "I know who you are. Your writing is awesome." Max grimaced and thanked Dr. Saul's famous daughter.

RED ROCK

Winter/Spring 1990, Age 28: Max was sure she was going to lose her children in a custody battle. She was also sure she would commit suicide when she lost custody. She was experiencing these lonely, painful feelings as she looked into the fireplace at a friend's mountain home.

The woman in red heard a voice come out of the fire. It said, "You have a strong fire in your heart, like a red rock. You will not lose your children." Immediately Max felt better.

The day of the trial, the woman in red was so terrified she was shaking. The voice from the fire chanted inside her head, *Red rock, red rock, red rock.*

Her lawyer pulled Mason's lawyer aside, and Mason's lawyer said they planned to use Max's father's being an alcoholic and Max's going to a coming out group in order to establish that she was lesbian. There was a sodomy law in North Carolina at the time, and it was illegal to have a same sex partner. The woman in red's lawyer had said earlier in his office that if Max said she had a girlfriend the case would be turned over to a constitutional judge. All the constitutional judges were conservative and would take the children away from the woman in red and throw Max in jail. The judge handling the case, who was not a constitutional judge, was about to retire. He had seen everything. He would understand that Mason was trying to use the sodomy law. Max had told Mason she was in love with Macy but she had never admitted to having sex with Macy. Max wanted to proclaim to the whole world that she loved Macy, emotionally, physically, and spiritually. But she didn't want to lose her children.

On the stand, the woman in red could feel the judge's gaze on her. She was shaking in fear. Max had made a chart showing that Mason took the children for nap time and night bedtime. She had the children for more waking hours than Mason.

Mason's lawyer asked if the father of the woman in red was an alcoholic. Max said he had been to rehab recently and was a recovering alcoholic. Then came the big question. "Is it true that you went to a coming out group to find out that you are lesbian?"

"I went to a coming out group, but I found out that I am not lesbian." The woman in red figured she was bisexual and that she was not lying. Of course being bisexual wasn't something she said out loud. It would also send her to a constitutional judge.

The judge sitting next to her breathed a heavy sigh. "I've heard enough. You can step down."

When the woman in red had taken her seat next to her lawyer, the judge declared, "I rule in favor of the mother." Max's heart was in shock. She had won!

As she and her lawyer walked by Mason and his lawyer, Mason hissed, "You lied."

The woman in red said nothing.

She was still afraid of Mason and would remain so for years to come.

HOUSES

February 1990-Fall 1991, Ages 28-30: Macy lived with two other women. They were just friends, not lovers. The nerdy woman lived in the attic section of the shared bungalow. She was very proud of her cozy attic.

Two months into their relationship, the woman in red took Zeb and Sarah with her to visit Macy in her attic. For some reason, the nerdy woman's street was blocked off. Max parked the car near the roadblock and saw heavy smoke in the sky. The woman in red thought, *I swear that looks like the smoke is coming from Macy's house.* As Max and the children moved closer to the smoke, they saw that it was the nerdy woman's house that was on fire. Macy and her housemates were watching from the front lawn. Big tears were rolling down the nerdy woman's face. She barely acknowledged the woman in red. Max stood beside her lover and watched until the fire fighters were gone. They said the two lawn mowers were too close to the old furnace in the basement. The mowers exploded and the flames shot straight up to the attic.

Macy needed somewhere to stay until she and her housemates found a new place to live. The nerdy woman moved in with the woman in red at the daddy's house. But the fire changed her. Macy spent hours on the phone talking to old friends, and then she would tell Max how wonderful all her friends were.

After several days of this, the woman in red sat the nerdy woman down and stammered, "You you spend all your time talking to all these other folks. You ignore me, except to tell me about your friends being there for you. My father and I have provided you with a place to stay, but you show no thanks for that. I want you to move out."

Max expected Macy to argue. Instead, the nerdy woman broke down and cried, "I'm sorry. You are right. I have been horrible to you. It's just that the fire has shaken me to my core. I lost almost every material possession I own. I guess I felt safer reconnecting with the old instead of connecting to the new. You are my new love. I guess I unconsciously decided I would lose you, too. I promise I won't ignore you any more. I am truly thankful that you have given me a place to stay. Please don't kick me out."

The woman in red was shocked that Macy agreed with her. Max was quiet for a long time. Finally, she said, "You can stay as long as you change for the better."

"I will. I promise."

The nerdy woman did an about face. She cherished her lover, while she looked for a new place with her housemates. By the end of the week, they had found a new space.

A year later, the nerdy woman and the woman in red decided to move in together. They went about the task of finding a downstairs duplex for themselves and Zeb and Sarah. It had a giant backyard for the kids. After a few months, Max realized her children didn't really like to go outside. She was sorely disappointed.

The woman in red cautiously said to Macy, "I don't know what you think about this, but I feel like I need my own bedroom. I want my own space."

"Tell me more."

"I've gone from one relationship to another. I don't want to suffocate."

The nerdy woman responded calmly, "Well, I've never lived with a lover before. So I am more than happy to have my own bedroom."

So Max took the largest room and made it her bedroom. Macy took two small, adjoining rooms and called it her suite.

The children were given the second biggest room. Zeb slept on the top bunk, and Sarah took the bottom. They were four and three years old.

It wasn't long before the nerdy woman felt overwhelmed by her instant family. She had explosive fights with the woman in red. Eventually the nerdy woman began to heal in analysis and let go of her rage from her past. She learned to walk away and cool down when she got mad at Max.

The woman in red always wanted to resolve arguments right away. She had to learn to let Macy have her space and time away. Max had to get out of the nerdy woman's face. There were residual effects each month when Macy had PMS. The woman in red worried her lover would lose it again, and then the couple would lose their special relationship. Here was a relationship both had dreamed of, but it could be lost so easily.

The fights were about emotional space, who was forcing whom to do what. The more they talked, the more they realized neither woman was pushing her will on the other. It was projection that made them believe the worst in each other. The women agreed that each of them should remain in individual therapy and work on each woman's issues. Their fights were more about their past than their present. In the present, they became each other's best cheerleader. As that first year of cohabitating came to an end, so did the fights.

BROKEN LEG

Leg broke in Spring 1981, Age 29: While Max was working on a concrete floor, she felt and heard a pop in her left knee. She had never had problems with that knee before. From that moment on, the left knee of the woman in red hurt. She went from doctor to doctor. None of them could figure out what was wrong because nothing was torn or broken. Finally, Max ended up in Dr. Paul Meyer's office. He looked young, and he was really excited. "I know what is wrong! Your leg bone is pushed into your kneecap. I've been working on a surgery to separate the two. But let's be cautious. I'll do a patella release and see if the knee cap will move on its own."

The patella release did not work. The woman in red was still in pain. A year and a half later, a more extensive surgery was performed with cut bone and screws. A week after surgery, Max was watching both Macy and the children practice soccer on fields right next to each other. The woman in red decided to move a little closer to the fields to get a better view. She had been told she could put weight on her leg while on her crutches. Max hobbled on her crutches, and all of a sudden, she felt and heard a crack in her leg. She fell to the ground in excruciating pain. The ground felt like a block of ice that drained all of the woman in red's body heat. Cindy, the women's soccer coach, took charge. She put coats on top of Max and talked to her in a calm voice. Somebody called 911.

X-rays showed that the woman in red had pulled out the screws from the surgery and had broken the tibia, the larger of the two bones between the knee and ankle, into two long sheets. Dr. Meyer was skiing in Colorado. Max would have to wait with an unset bone. When Dr. Meyer came back to town, he said, "I can fix it!"

A week after the incident, the woman in red was back in surgery. Not only did the knee need to be operated on again, the tibia had to be screwed back together up and down the bone. Recovery was long and painful. Max was depressed for many months, as her leg healed slowly. She had very little energy, and she slept a lot. A year after the operation, the screws in the tibia were trying to push up through the skin. The woman in red would go back to surgery to remove the screws. Fortunately, that was minor surgery.

Max would not want to repeat the year for anything.

COPY MACHINES

1st copy shop job – Fall 1990-Fall 1991, 2nd copy shop job – Fall 1991-Fall 1993, 3rd copy shop job – February 2003-February 2004: Max needed a job. She walked into the copy shop and was hired immediately because she said she would work the graveyard shift from midnight to 8 a.m. The woman in red loved working with the giant copy machines. She did not like working with the public. It totally drained Max to deal with people face to face. Fortunately, there weren't a lot of customers in the early morning hours. But the graveyard shift made her lonely and depressed. Macy and the kids were awake when the woman in red was asleep and vice versa.

After a year, she moved to another copy shop where she could work the day shift. At the second copy shop, Max was in charge of big production projects. She loved her machines so much that she talked to them and gave them names. She called the biggest and fastest machine Rabun. The woman in red could swear that Rabun had a soul, and she could hear its heart beat. (Rabun was neither male nor female.)

Max figured God put perfect souls into God's perfect creation. Since humans mimic God, humans put less than perfect souls into their less than perfect creations, like copy machines. She borrowed the idea from the Thomist philosopher, Jacques Maritain. He was talking about artists and their artwork. The woman in red just extended the idea to inventors and their machines.

Max had such a good production track record that soon everybody on staff was talking to Rabun and the other machines to try to copy the success of the woman in red.

Max also talked to her washing machine and dryer at home. She painted faces on them and named them Riley and Mattie.

After two years at the second copy shop, the woman in red quit to take a part-time job as an after-school teacher. That way, she could work with her children and have more time to study for her second Masters degree. After several years as an after school teacher, she became a hospital chaplain for five years.

Then she went back to another copy shop. The copy machines had become more complicated with computer technology. Max preferred the finishing machines. There was the giant cutter, the folding machine, the laminators, the booklet maker, and the business card maker. The woman in red loved the predictability of these machines. She loved having her handiwork praised. She would leave that job to become a hospice chaplain. But Max would not forget her love for machines.

SARAH'S THERAPY

Summer 1991, Age 29: Mason rarely saw the children. When he did, he dropped them at the curb, instead of walking them to the door. One time, Zeb walked in, but Sarah stayed outside the door. She was sitting on the ground. Max asked why she didn't come in.

Sarah said her feet were bleeding and that she would bleed on the carpet if she came in. The woman in red looked at Sarah's feet. They looked fine, but her daughter was not talking fine. Max was frightened and called Macy to the door. Sarah told Macy that she couldn't come inside because her feet were bleeding.

Macy picked up Sarah and said matter-of-factly, "You can bleed all over the house if you wish. It doesn't bother me."

Another day when the woman in red was working in a small town in North Carolina, and Macy was home alone with the children, the nerdy woman noticed that it was really quiet. She walked around the house and found four-year-old Sarah with the cord to the blinds wrapped around her neck. She was turning blue. Macy found scissors in a hurry and cut the cord. She put Sarah in the child's bed and then ran to the backyard and screamed. When the nerdy woman had calmed down, she asked Sarah if she was playing.

Sarah said, "My daddy doesn't think I am pretty. That is why he doesn't come to see me." When Macy told Max about Sarah hanging herself, the woman in red felt helpless and very discouraged. She was frightened for her daughter. Sarah had other symptoms of being out of control. She threw screaming fits every time Max and Macy tried to take her anywhere. Sarah also spilled milk and juice at least three times a week, and she kept stepping on the feet of the woman in red.

The nerdy woman had a therapist friend named Riley who worked with children. He said Sarah felt helpless. He let Sarah make big messes with paint. Riley also made up games where Sarah got to tell him what to do. For example she rode on his shoulders and told him where to walk. He also lifted her upside down and let her walk on the ceiling. Slowly Sarah got better. Her screaming fits became less and less. She didn't try to harm herself or talk of bleeding feet any more. She stopped knocking over her milk and stopped stepping on Max's feet. She began to put her hands in Macy and the woman in red's hands and say with glee, "We're the girls."

In a year, Sarah didn't need therapy any more. Macy said she was the most well adjusted in the family.

THE BUMP

Fall 1991, Age 30: Sarah, who was four, had strep throat three times in a row. A bump came up on her neck when the third round of antibiotics finished. The doctors thought the bump was a rare form of tuberculosis and that they would have to remove a part of Sarah's throat. The doctors took a biopsy and gave strict orders not to bother the nodule while they grew cultures. If the bump came open, Max was supposed to take Sarah straight to the emergency room.

For three weeks, everything went fine until one of the cats scratched the bump. Max and Macy took Sarah to the E.R. The biopsies were back. Sarah did not have tuberculosis. The emergency room doctor strapped Sarah down and slit open the nodule. Infection came out. Sarah screamed and wriggled under the straps. The woman in red felt helpless, as the doctor pressed on the bump and more infection came out. Eventually, it was all over. Sarah would not be losing a part of her throat, but she would have scar on her throat the rest of her life where the doctor removed the infection.

SOCCER

Fall 1991-Spring 1996, Ages 30-35: Macy was on a women's thirty and over soccer team. She played sweeper on defense. When Max turned thirty and had been with the nerdy woman two years, she joined the team. Since she couldn't run fast because of her knee surgeries, plus she was good at catching a ball, the woman in red became a goalie. She absolutely loved flying sideways through the air to stop the ball. When there was mud, Max rolled in it before the game started so she would not be afraid of it during the game. The woman in red had a hard time understanding the concept of game time, which was usually different from her internal clock. She would tell Macy she didn't want to play in the game. Macy would say, "I'll buy you a cherry frozen drink if you'll play today." Max had loved frozen drinks since she was a little girl. So she would play to get the drink. After she started moving around on the field, the woman in red liked playing very much. She would soar through the air and roll on the ground, anything to get the ball. Sometimes she was an awesome player. Sometimes Max was only average. No matter what, she had fun.

Nobody is supposed to touch the goalie. It she does she gets a penalty. The woman in red had learned years before in basketball camp how to ham it up. So if she were barely touched, she would fall to the ground, screaming like she was in pain. This made it so the referee didn't miss the illegal contact. The only problem was that Macy would believe Max was really hurt. Poor Macy. She would fall for the acting of the woman in red every time. Sometimes there was a real concern when Max would get kicked in the head. There was no faking getting knocked out. After five years, the woman in red quit soccer because it was too dangerous to risk getting kicked in the head again.

In the meantime, Zeb and Sarah were five and six, old enough to play soccer. They did not play goalie and risk getting kicked in the head. The woman in red volunteered to be their coach for many years. She got along great with the kids on her teams. Most parents were wonderful, but some drove Max crazy with their doubting questions of why she was doing certain things. The main technique besides teaching basic skills was praising each member of the team as often as possible. It worked on many of the children, and a losing team became a winning team every time.

Like in everything else, Zeb and Sarah were opposite in the way they played. Zeb was a gifted player who soared during practice. Zeb loved scrimmage. He was beautiful to watch. But he felt too much pressure during games and would beg not to play. Zeb barely touched the ball during game time. Sarah, on the other hand, was not a gifted player at first. She had to work hard for every skill she learned. To begin with, her only skill was dribbling, and she did that slowly. Sarah saw no reason for practice. She said it was boring. But come game time, she begged to play. "Put me in. I'll get the ball." Out of shear heart, Sarah would end up with the ball time and time again. She would dribble a little bit and then be run over by the other team. A few minutes later, she would have the ball again. Over the years, Sarah became a great passer. She stayed with soccer until playing the viola took up her spare time in junior high.

THERAPY WITH JEAN

Fall 1992-Present, Ages 31-56: "Do you still like me?" the woman in red asked her new therapist every ten minutes, to counteract the criticism in her soul left behind by her parents. She continued to criticize herself long after being in her parents' care.

Sheila had not been able to continue therapy. Max was brokenhearted. For a few years, the woman in red worked with different therapists at NC, but they were in training and left after a year or two. Lexie, the last of Max's GSU therapists, recommended Jean Hayes. Jean had a calm, positive presence that counteracted the anxiety and depression of the woman in red. At first, Max could barely look Jean in the eye. Slowly, she began to look into a most welcoming gaze. Jean' eyes smiled back at the woman in red. Every ten minutes, she would look in Jean' eyes and ask, "Do you still like me?" She braced herself for a blow. Max was used to criticism, first from her parents and then from herself. Her parents liked to comment on her differences from other children. First, the little girl in red and now, the woman in red received all those comments as criticism. But Jean was not a critical person. She was loving and warm. She found that Max needed to give and receive love, just like everybody else on the planet.

It would take many years for the woman in red to love herself, for it took baby steps to get there.

"Do you still like me?"

"Yes."

Baby step.

A year into therapy with Jean, Lexie (the therapist) was setting up her own practice. She had been in training in California and was returning to Charlotte. Max had to choose whether or not to stay with Jean.

Jean usually let the woman in red start each session. But the therapist spoke first one session when she said, "We need to talk."

"Okay," responded Max.

"I know Lexie is coming back to town to set up practice. I just wanted to say I wish you would continue to see me. I think we have a good thing going."

In that moment the woman, in red felt special and chosen. She answered, "You do?"

"Yes, I think we make a good team."

Max looked into Jean' eyes for the first time that session. Jean looked serious. The woman in red mumbled, "Wow."

"You can take time to think about it."

"I don't need time."

"So, you know what you will do?"

Max looked at her toes. "I'll stay with you."

"I'm glad."

The woman in red peeked at her therapist. Jean was smiling. Max grimaced.

Some years later, the woman in red couldn't get enough of Jean. Max would say, "How about we run down to Mexico and get away from it all?"

"What will we do there?" asked Jean.

"Absolutely nothing. We can lie out on the beach, jump the waves, get massages, and eat steak and shrimp."

"Sounds wonderful."

It took a very long time, but eventually, Max didn't want to run away with Jean to Mexico. She felt the warmth and embrace of the fifty-minute hour.

After more years, the woman in red made a great breakthrough and asked for a hug. She had given and received hugs from Mason and Macy, but they were mostly before and after sex. Rarely did Max give or receive a hug out of nowhere.

"I want to ask for something I've never asked from you before." The woman in red struggled to look Jean in the eye.

"What is it?"

"A hug," Max almost whispered.

"What would a hug mean to you?"

"It would be a physical confirmation of the love and acceptance I get from you. You know I don't let very many people hug me. I don't even let Macy hug me very often. I've had a lonely existence, cut off from the people who love me. I know how to have sex, but I don't know how to just stay in touch with the people around me. I missed out a lot on life. So, can I get a hug from you?"

"Yes."

That hug was an opening of a door for the woman in red. She hugged Macy more after that. It wasn't a radical change, more like a quiet rain on an autumn day. It was peaceful and soothing.

Jean began putting her hand on Max's back, as the woman in red left therapy.

"Why do you put your hand on my back when I leave?" Max asked in the middle of a session.

"Why do you think?"

"It's another way you convey that you like me."

"Yes. Does it bother you?"

"It would have in the past. Now I've come to expect it from you. I feel connected to you as I go out into the world."

Counteracting the lonely childhood of the woman in red remains the main reason for therapy. There is a loneliness at her very core from not being held and barely talking as a child. Connecting first to Jean and then to the rest of the world combats the loneliness. But participating in the world around her is taxing to Max's soul. It is much easier to keep to herself. But Jean keeps coaxing Max out of her introverted stance.

Jean reiterates every so often, "We make a good team because we work well together."

The woman in red agrees, "Yes we do."

MACY AND THE CHILDREN

Max and Macy moved in together – March 1991, Zeb wrote note – Summer of 1996: Zeb and Sarah had pole opposite reactions to having Macy in their lives. Sarah loved her. Zeb hated her. Sarah missed her father, and she filled a part of that hole with the new grownup in her life. She was smitten. Sarah didn't seem to notice that the nerdy woman and her mother were a couple. As far as Sarah was concerned, Macy was her woman. In preschool, Sarah was asked to paint a member of her family. She painted a woman with long orange hair. The nerdy woman didn't have long hair, but Sarah thought it looked good on the love of her life. The preschool teacher asked who was in the painting. Sarah exclaimed, "That's *my* Macy!"

Zeb, on the other hand, was a mama's boy. He didn't miss Mason as much as Sarah did. But he sure as hell didn't expect to get rid of one rival in his father to be replaced by a woman, of all things. Zeb simply ignored the nerdy woman as much as possible. He only had eyes for Max. There was a show with Muppets in it called *The Dinosaurs*. The baby dinosaur called the father "Not the Mama." When his mother came in the room, the baby dinosaur squealed with delight, "It's the MAMA!" Zeb mimicked the show all the time. "It's the Mama!" he would announce with passion each day after school let out.

Zeb and Macy had some similarities. They were seriously into wristwatches, and they both loved the Charlotte, NC baseball team. Zeb's watch broke when he was with his father. Mason and the kids got back to Max and the nerdy woman's place before the couple got back. By the time the woman in red and Macy came home, the kids were asleep in bed. On the nerdy woman's bed was a note from Zeb that said, "Dear Macy my watch broke, so I borrowed one of yours. I knew you would understand." It took many years of constant love from Macy towards "the boy," as she affectionately called Zeb. Finally, Zeb had reached out to the nerdy woman and trusted her. With that one note, they crossed a line of affection for each other. For years after that, they could be seen watching baseball on television together. Sometimes they went to the stadium and watched a game in the heat.

CATS

Duplo gets sick – Summer of 1992, Age 31: Max and Macy loved cats. They had as many as five at one time. Zeb was gentle with the cats, and the cats loved him. Sarah chased the cats, and they ran from her. Engine, who had been found in the engine of a neighbor's car, was too fat to get away. Sarah would scoop up the gray tabby and hug her tight. Engine would scratch and claw to get away, but the girl hung on tight. Engine got her revenge at night. After Sarah fell asleep, Engine would pull her fat self up into the girl's loft bed. Then the cat would push Sarah's head off her pillow. Triumphant, Engine claimed the pillow as her throne. When Max saw this, she scooted the cat off the bed. In no time Engine was sitting pretty on Sarah's pillow again.

Zeb also had a cat. He was a yellow striped cat named Duplo, after Duplo building blocks both children played with. Duplo was a rough and tumble kind of cat. One rainy day, the woman in red announced a new game called cat-bowling, a game Duplo would come to love. She balled up the cats and slid them on their backs down the big hall in their duplex. The four girl cats ran away and hid after one bowl. But Duplo came back for more and more. From then on, cat-bowling meant sliding Duplo on the floor until the cat got dizzy and fell over. He acted drunk, and he purred with bliss.

One summer day, Zeb announced that Duplo was permanently flopped over next to his food bowl. This was very unlike the active cat. The woman in red and Macy took Duplo to the veterinarian. The vet ran expensive tests that told the couple nothing. Did they want to pay $1000 for exploratory surgery?

The nerdy woman said, "We don't have that kind of money. We will take him home to die." So they placed Duplo next to his food and water bowls.

Each morning Zeb could be heard speaking to his cat. "Are you dead yet, Honey?"

After a month, the first breeze of autumn blew through the kitchen window and Duplo popped up. The house didn't have airconditioning, and it seemed that Zeb's cat was an airconditioning cat. The next summer Duplo fell out again when it got too hot. But the next year, the family moved to an airconditioned apartment, and Duplo never suffered again.

DR. LINDETAL

Fall 1992, Age 31: Dr. Heinrick Lindetal was used to being feared. Max had always been terrible at memorizing. She preferred not to see the German-born professor's wrath, so she rattled off the Biblical Hebrew verb charts that he demanded. She was taking an independent study course from the esteemed professor.

"So you think you know the Qal perfect. Then let's start on the Qal imperfect right now," Dr. Lindetal frowned.

The woman in red smiled.

"Why are you smiling? I usually make women cry."

"Because this is the best I have ever done. I am doing well for me," Max continued, smiling.

"Hmm. We shall see. Read out the verbs on the chart."

They continued their one-on-one session until Dr. Lindetal's British wife, interrupted for a tea break.

"She doesn't deserve any," barked the professor.

"Oh, Hedrick, everybody deserves a tea break," Mrs. Lindetal said in an upbeat, sing-song way. She left the student and teacher to their tea and chocolate cake.

"Do you like the cake?" Dr. Lindetal interrogated.

"Yes, it is very tasty," the woman in red admitted.

"I made it."

"You did?"

"Don't act so surprised. I can follow a recipe. I'll give you a copy so you can make it for your children. I'll send home two pieces of cake for them, too. I shouldn't punish them, just because you are slow at Hebrew. When you finish your tea and cake, we will start on translation."

In the middle of translating Hebrew into English, Dr. Lindetal sighed, "I'll be dead by the time you figure this out. I'm 78, and I don't think I'll celebrate very many more birthdays."

They met at Dr. Lindetal's house twice a week for four months. Dr. Lindetal was always strict and wore a frown. Max continued to smile at her progress. This was the advanced Biblical Hebrew she had asked for. The registrar from the small seminary sent her across the street from the seminary to the retired Dr. Lindetal's house. The woman in red was afraid at first, but she believed the professor cared about her, underneath his stern appearance.

Near the end of the semester, Dr. Lindetal said during tea break, "Wait here. I have something to show you." He brought out an ancient piece of paper with big red letters that spelled "JUDEN." "You see I was raised by Christians who adopted me. Hitler made everybody look up his or her ancestry. When they looked up mine they found out I had Jewish birth parents. That is why my passport is stamped "JUDEN." My adoptive parents sneaked me out of Germany in a trunk. I ended up with an English couple. Now you know my story."

Over the last sessions, Dr. Lindetal told Max more. He said he took college exams in England by doing independent study since the colleges were shut down because of the war. And he told how he got into the Old Testament Ph.D. program at Princeton because he knew German, not Hebrew. It was assumed he could learn Hebrew since he already knew two languages.

Finally, the day came for the woman in red to turn in her take-home exam. Dr. Lindetal graded it in front of her. She got everything right on her translation.

The professor looked up with tearful eyes. "What is this cranky old man going to do without you as his student?"

Max remedied the situation. She found other languages to learn from Dr. Lindetal. She would learn Aramaic, Advanced Biblical Greek, and German reading.

Dr. Lindetal died a few years later. The woman in red would miss her cranky old man.

GHOST

Fall 1993, Age 32: One night on her way home from work, Max heard a female voice say, "Check on your father." The woman in red couldn't say whether the voice was in her head or outside her head. She was alone in the car, but she didn't question the voice because it held an urgency. She would check on her father in the morning. The daddy was drinking again and had been evicted from his apartment for not paying his rent. He lived in a hotel on a dangerous street.

The next morning, the woman in red went to the hotel and knocked on the daddy's door. The voice behind the door said, "Go away."

"What's going on?" Max demanded from her side of the door.

The spirit of death crept under the door. The woman in red felt a chill go down her spine. "I'm going to kill myself at the end of the day. I have it all planned out," said her father.

Max thought, *I have time. I need to get help.* She said aloud, "I'll be back. Don't do anything."

The woman in red went home and called her brother-in-law Hugo, who was a mental health professional. He was married to Lila, aka My Baby. Hugo knew the number of a suicide hotline. He also said Max should not be alone with her father. He told her to get help from her brother Peter (also known as My Boy) or from Macy. Macy was out of town, so the woman in red called her brother. He was married to his work, so she didn't expect much from him. But Peter surprised her. He said he would be right over. Next, Max called the hotline and got someone called Lucy. Lucy instructed the woman in red to ask her father if he would accept help. If he said yes, she should call Lucy back, so she could talk to the daddy.

Peter arrived and drove Max to the hotel. He knocked on their father's door and demanded that it be opened. Slowly the door creaked open. All the lights were out. The daddy did not look his children in the eye.

"What's going on, Daddy?" asked Peter.

"I'm sure Max has told you."

"Do you want help?" asked the woman in red.

"Yes," their father replied.

They got Lucy on the line, who got the daddy to agree he would not do anything today to harm himself, and he would let the children take him to the public hospital's emergency room.

At Lenox Hill Hospital, the daddy saw a psychiatrist who started him on an antidepressant. Since he no longer planned to kill himself, the daddy was allowed to go back to his hotel room. The crisis was over.

When her brother drove her home, Max asked, "Why did you come so fast? That is not like you to leave your work."

"I saw Grandma Maxine's ghost," Peter replied matter-of-factly. Grandma Maxine was the dead mother of the daddy.

"You what?"

"Sasha (My Boy's wife) and I were fast asleep, when the cat started growling and woke us. A young woman's image stood in the corner. Sasha asked who that was. I said, 'That is my grandmother.' The ghost said to check on my father."

"And you didn't go directly to check on him?" the woman in red asked.

"I knew you would call."

"Hey," said Max. "Why did you get a ghost, and all that I got was a voice in my ear?"

"You have a stronger faith. It took a ghost to move me."

DR. BRUCKNER

Fall 1993, Age 32: William Bruckner was a famous Old Testament professor because he was well published. He was hidden away at a small Presbyterian seminary in a suburb of N.C,. Max had finished her Master of Divinity in May of 1992. She decided to go to a the small seminary to get a Master of Theology in Old Testament and to study under William Bruckner the next year. She only went part time and took five years to get a degree that usually takes one to two years to earn. She hoped to go on and get her PhD to become an Old Testament professor.

Dr. Bruckner was a rhetorical critic who stood in opposition to the historical critics of the bigger semiaries The historical critics tore the Bible apart by saying there were many writers and editors to any given piece of scripture. We can't be sure of the meaning because so many people are saying so many different things. The rhetorical critics accepted what the historical critics brought to the table but claimed there is meaning in the completed story. They found that certain rhetoric was repeated and that there was much to learn from the way the completed stories are told.

William Bruckner had a big, booming, charismatic voice. He opened class with prayer, and it felt like the heavens opened for him. Somehow he knew the woman in red had gone to one of the big seminaires. So when she raised her hand and asked, "How do you know that really happened?" Dr. Bruckner thought he was looking at a historical critic. Max was not a historical critic. She just thought the professor could help her answer the historical critics.

William Bruckner blew up. He yelled at the woman in red. Max did nothing. She just sat there and listened to Dr. Bruckner say everything he wanted to say to the historical critics. William Bruckner had always been long winded. He was extra so, as he huffed and puffed and let it all out. Eventually, he caught himself and looked around the stunned room. Then he started to apologize.

The woman in red felt her eyes mist. *I am not going to cry*, she thought to herself. *I wish I could disappear. Why won't he be quiet?*

William Bruckner called an end to class. Max shuffled out the door.

What am I going to do now? How can I finish this degree when I don't want to go back to class? After a couple of hours of fretting, she called her old academic advisor from the big seminary, Grayson Donaldson.

Dr. Donaldson didn't sound surprised to hear from her. In fact she seemed already to know what had happened.

The woman in red said, "He called you, didn't he?"

"Yes. And what I want to know is why didn't you fight back? You took on professors."

"I don't know. What do I do now?"

"You work it out. You are both smart people. I have faith in you."

Max called Dr. Bruckner's secretary and made an appointment for the next day. William Bruckner had a large office with books all around. He started apologizing again before the woman in red had even sat down. Dr. Bruckner said he would recommend her to whatever school she wanted to attend for her doctorate.

When he finally got quiet Max complained, "You are always going to remember me because you yelled at me, not because of my work."

"You're right," the professor agreed.

When there was nothing else to say, the woman in red left the famous man's office.

After that day, Max took a lot of classes from William Bruckner. He was a very thorough teacher. He knew a great deal about the Old Testament. Sometimes the woman in red fought with him. One day, he shook her desk to get his point across. Max stood up, put her hands on her hips, and said, "I don't see why the Israelites should listen to Yaweh."

"Because he is GOD!"

"Even God should behave."

Whether she was talking about the God of the Old Testament or Dr.Bruckner, the woman in red had come a long way from the day she just sat there and took it.

BIRTHDAY PARTY

March 1994, Age 32: When Sarah was about to turn seven, she figured out that every one that came to a birthday party brought a present. Therefore, she wanted the biggest party ever. Sarah invited her soccer team and kids from her first grade class. She invited grown-up friends of Max and Macy. She even invited Grayson Donaldson, the woman in red's academic advisor from her seminary days. Max didn't have a lot of money, so she asked every family to bring a covered dish. Sarah and Zeb had a lot of toys and a big backyard. They set up play areas all over the backyard. There was a G.I. Joe area, a Barbie area, a Ninja Turtle area, and a Hot Wheels area. Because the woman in red had already spoiled the children with toys, she told Sarah to give away her better looking old toys to the children who came to the party.

The weather was perfect. Everybody who was invited came. The play areas were a big success. Even Dr. Donaldson showed up. There was plenty to eat. Sarah blew out her candles. Near the end of the party, Mason, the ex-husband of the woman in red, showed up and held Sarah in his lap. Sarah was very happy to see her dad, but it was difficult for Max to be around Mason because she was still afraid of him.

The crowd and the entire event wore out Max, but she was happy for her daughter.

SARAH AND GLORIA STEINEM

Spring 1994, Age 32: When Sarah was seven the famous feminist, Gloria Steinem, gave a talk and signed her most recent book, *Moving Beyond Words*, at the local feminist bookstore. When Max explained that Ms. Steinem had helped women get more money in the workplace, Sarah exclaimed, "She's like Susan B. Anthony, who helped women vote."

"Yes, she is like that," confirmed the woman in red.

Max worried that Gloria Steinem's speech would go over Sarah's head. But Sarah sat up straight and listened intently. When Ms. Steinem finished speaking and sat down to sign books, Sarah asked her mother, "If Gloria Steinem is so important, why isn't she the President of the United States?"

The woman in red was worn out because she had been to the annual gay pride celebration most of the day. She simply said, "I don't know. Why don't you ask her?"

Sarah was too young to read Ms. Steinem's book, so Max pulled a copy of *The Secret Garden* off the children's bookshelf. Even though Gloria Steinem had not written it, perhaps she would sign the book for Sarah. So Sarah hopped in line with the grownups and waited her turn to ask Ms. Steinem a question. When it was Sarah's turn to get her book signed, the bookstore's co-owner, Lisa Basil, knew Sarah and introduced her to Gloria Steinem.

The woman in red piped up and said, "Sarah has a question for you."

Ms. Steinem was sitting at a small table. She signed *The Secret Garden* and looked the seven-year-old in the eye. "What is your question?"

Sarah didn't hesitate. "Why haven't there been any women presidents?"

Gloria Steinem answered, "This country hasn't been fair to women. But when you are old enough, you can run for president, and I will help you."

"Okay," Sarah responded.

On the way home, Max's daughter said nothing of her encounter with the famous feminist. But just before she got into bed she said to her mother in a worried tone, "We probably won't live here when I run for president. How will Gloria Steinem find me?"

The woman in red said in a reassuring voice, "If you run for president, Gloria Steinem *will* find you."

Max and Sarah didn't discuss the matter again until a year later. It was time for Sarah to graduate from picture books and start reading chapter books. It wasn't something that came naturally for Sarah, and she wasn't eager to start the process. She asked her mother out of the blue, "Does the President of the United States have to be able to read chapter books?"

"Yes," the woman in red smiled.

"Dog."

The next year, Sarah ran for a student office position and lost. Max was frightened that her daughter would be crushed. But Sarah pushed out her lip and announced, "All those people who didn't vote for me are going to regret it when I become President of the United States."

Sarah never mentioned the presidency again. But the woman in red is eternally grateful to Gloria Steinem.

CARDS, STUFFED ANIMALS, AND A PAINTING

Max and Macy wrote love notes in cards with women's artwork on the front that they had bought from the feminist bookstore. The woman in red wrote lengthy passages, listing all the reasons she loved the nerdy woman. She would list romantic trips to the mountains or the beach that the two of them took alone. Max reminded Macy of conversations about the possibility of being "star children" from another part of the universe. The nerdy woman had read that some babies were dropped on this planet from an advanced race that was interested in learning more about this lonely outpost called Earth. These star children could recognize each other by looking into one another's eyes. They didn't quite fit in their Earth skin. When Macy called the woman in red a fellow star child, Max felt special. All the woman in red had to write on a card was "star children" and that special feeling came back.

The nerdy woman also claimed that, spiritually, she was like an excited little bird, mixed with a wise, slow-moving turtle. Max found a children's stuffed animal that reminded her of Macy. It was a bird with Amelia Earhart flying goggles and flying cap. She named it Little Bird and put it on Macy's bed to surprise her. The nerdy woman's response to such a wonderful gift was to go back to the card shop to find a stuffed monkey with red eyes that reminded her of Max. She named the monkey Redrock, after the voice in the fire that said to the woman in red, "You have a strong fire in your heart, like a red rock." Little Bird and Redrock sat on Macy's bed with their arm and wing around one another.

When Sarah was about five, she claimed Redrock as her own and took her to her bed. She kept the stuffed animal until she moved out of the house at age eighteen. Max received the much loved monkey back into her own arms and thought of days gone by.

Every once in a while the woman in red liked to paint. One Valentine's Day she painted the nerdy woman. It just seemed to Max that she should show Macy with a painting how much she loved the nerdy woman. The style was primitive, with bright colors, and Macy loved it. Max framed that painting and put it on the wall, where it still is today.

ODDS AND ENDS

One of the reasons Max and Macy got along so well was that they were both introverts. They could spend hours on opposite ends of their apartment and not feel neglected. The nerdy woman could read all day with cats curled on and around her. The woman in red always had some home improvement or writing project going. When the children were young, they played with their toys and read their books. As they got older, they played on the computer and talked on the phone in their rooms.

The couple also got along because they agreed to disagree theologically. For Macy, God was love. This was too abstract for Max. For her, God was the person of Jesus, with whom she could talk. The nerdy woman was not a big fan of Jesus, but she was glad the woman in red got so much out of him. What Macy did like to discuss with Max was the topic of the female spirit. The woman in red first heard the female spirit in a giant rock on a camping trip with the nerdy woman. As the years went by, she heard the same spirit in the wind, in giant trees, and on the ocean. Each time, the spirit encouraged Max to be her best self. It felt like heaven was cheering for her.

As far as chores went, Macy was the grocery shopper and cook. She didn't make complicated dishes, which pleased the children. Max was in charge of the children's schedule and discipline. She also bought their clothes, toys, and books. The woman in red was both strict at times with

Zeb and Sarah, and at times, spoiled them with a lot of toys that made them happy.

The nerdy woman insisted on vacations. She took Max and the kids to the beach, where Sarah splashed in the waves and Zeb dug in the sand. She also took them to her parents' property in the Kentucky mountains with a river running through it. Macy insisted that they go camping. She loved to camp. One of her favorite spots to take the children and Max was in one of the Creeks in Georgia because they could ride inner tubes in the water. At the creek, Zeb and Sarah got to help set up their own tent and help cook over a fire. Mostly they liked throwing rocks into the creek. They did that for hours.

At the Wilderness in the North Carolina mountains, the nerdy woman said they all had to backpack a mile to an island where they were going to stay. The children had their light sleeping bags, two pairs of thin soccer shorts, two tank tops, and underwear in their small packs. Though it was light on their backs, it looked like the women were abusing the children. Sarah complained the whole way in, and people stopped her and gave her food and drink. They glared at Macy and the woman in red. Once they had crossed the river and made it to the island, the children were happy to splash in the water near the island's beach.

Max and the nerdy woman loved women's sports and women's concerts. They watched live women's professional basketball and women's soccer as often as they could afford it. They took the children to watch women's field hockey at the Olympics in Charlotte, NC. The couple loved seeing Melissa Etheridge and the Artic Women in concert. Their other favorites were Nanci Griffith, Iris Dement, and Mary Chapin Carpenter.

Halloween was a special time for the nerdy woman and the children. Max was afraid of Halloween, but Macy really got into it and loved helping the children with their costumes. Pretend monsters felt like real monsters to the woman in red.

Christmas meant car tracks and G.I. Joes for Zeb, and Barbies and American Girl dolls for Sarah. One year, Barbie got a pink limousine with plenty of room for her friends. Sarah played with that car for years.

Even though it was unusual for Zeb and Sarah to be raised by two women in a lesbian relationship in the southern part of the United States, their home lives were actually pretty much like other kids.

LEARNING TO WRITE

Fall 1995, Age 34: Max had to write two 20-page papers for her Master of Theology in Old Testament degree at a Theological Seminary. She had received mostly B's and an occasional C on her papers when she was working on her M.Div. degree, so she was intimidated by the assignment.

Katie Keplar had recently joined the Old Testament staff at Crafton. The woman in red approached Dr. Keplar and told her how she needed to learn how to write. The professor took on the challenge. The paper they worked on would count as one of the required 20 page papers.

Max wanted to write about the second chapter of the book of Hosea. A husband rants about how he plans to punish his adulterous wife. The wife never speaks. The husband and wife represent God and Israel. The woman in red claimed the words were abusive, whether they were spoken by a husband or by God.

As a feminist, Katie Keplar believed it was important to tell how Max's life connected with the text. The woman in red wrote about Dr. Bruckner yelling at her while she sat silently, not defending herself. Dr. Keplar said that all writing is crap when it comes to the table. She said not to expect praise, but for every little bit that you get, it is wonderful. When she read the first draft of Max's paper, Katie Keplar said great things about the writing, and at the same time, she marked through much of it with a red pen. She said the answer to how to become a good writer is to edit, edit, and edit some more. The woman in red had never edited her papers. She was frightened by so many words. Max would take the marked up paper and respond to the edits that Dr. Keplar wanted. She would turn the paper back in, and then they would repeat the process of praise and red pen markings.

The woman in red gained confidence in her writing as the paper improved. By the end of the semester, she had an A paper that could still be edited even more. She thanked Katie Keplar for her help. Dr. Keplar said she could thank her by teaching other women how to write.

Max Burke

STREET PERSON

1996, Age 34: The daddy had been in several detox units. He had run out of money, and he had lived with Peter, also known as My Boy, and Lila, also known as My Baby. But he wanted to continue to drink and verbally abuse the woman in red. He wanted to live with her. Instead, Max drove the daddy to the public hospital, to be detoxed yet again.

The next morning, the woman in red said to Macy, "He's here. My father is back. I can feel him. I can't breathe."

Macy thought Max was losing her mind." He's down at the hospital," she stated. "You took him last night."

"No, he is here! I can feel him."

They heard footsteps in the hall. "Hey, is anybody home?" called the daddy.

Macy was shocked. She walked out to the hall and asked the daddy what he was doing back.

"I checked myself out of the hospital. I didn't want their help."

"Well, you can't stay here. You are driving your daughter crazy." The nerdy woman was firm. Max was exhausted emotionally. She didn't have any more energy for her father.

The daddy turned back around and walked out the door. He refused to get help from the siblings of the woman in red. If the woman in red wouldn't let him live with her, he would become a street person. He went to the community kitchen where the woman in red used to work, and he got into the shelter just down the street from Max and Macy. The woman in red felt stalked. Peter told the daddy not to get any closer to Max.

The good news was that the Olympics were coming, and NC was cleaning up its streets. The daddy didn't get put in jail or run out of town, like most vagrants. A social worker found an apartment for the daddy in government housing. This probably happened because he was white and educated. He also started collecting Social Security for the first time.

Eventually the woman in red and the daddy made up. It wasn't a big dramatic moment. They just started seeing each other again. Max started taking the daddy grocery shopping every other Saturday. The daddy stopped drinking off and on. When he wasn't drinking, he was a sweet, kind man.

SINGING SARAH

Fall/Winter 1996, Age 35, Sarah was in fifth grade: When Sarah was in preschool, her class was going to sing for the holidays. The choir teacher said, "Sarah has the prettiest voice. I'm going to put her on the front row." Max had a gut feeling this might not end well, but she said nothing. As the children lined up for the performance, Sarah was looking at her toes. The music began, and Sarah did not open her mouth. Big crocodile tears fell down her face. The woman in red felt sorry for her little girl with the voice of an angel.

When Sarah was in public kindergarten, her teacher again thought she had discovered a great performer. Max thought of the Warner Brothers' singing frog cartoon. A man discovers a frog who can sing show tunes. He sees dollar signs from all the money he is going to make. When the curtain goes up on the big audience, the frog will only croak like a frog is supposed to do. Sarah would not sing in front of an audience. The woman in red told the teacher that Sarah had stage fright. The teacher assured Max that everything would be all right. When the performance took place yet again, Sarah didn't open her mouth, and tears were shed. The woman in red felt great pain for her daughter.

Sarah joined the school chorus in fifth grade. She was pretty sure she could sing in front of an audience by then. The chorus teacher told Max that Sarah should sing a solo for the holiday performance. The woman in red told the teacher about Sarah's younger years with stage fright. The chorus teacher said she had dealt with her own stage fright and that she could help Sarah get over hers.

Sarah had two solos the night of the holiday production. She had the singing solo, and she had a solo on her viola. Max had a hard time being in crowds. It was like she could hear every heartbeat. So she was in crowds as little as possible. Sarah said she would not be the first orchestra solo, so the woman in red showed up late to the performance. Only Sarah was wrong. She was the first solo. When she couldn't find her mother in the audience, Sarah had broken down crying. By the time Max showed up, her ex-husband Mason was kneeling in front of a sobbing Sarah. Both were at the front of the auditorium with the rest of the orchestra, for all to see. The woman in red marched down the aisle, took the crying child by the hand, and led her out of the auditorium to the girls' restroom. In the restroom, Sarah washed her face and calmed down.

Max said, "You have a choice. We can go home if you like, and I won't be ashamed of you. Or you can join the chorus production to sing your solo." Sarah surprised her by saying she wanted to sing. She hopped in line just before the chorus went on stage.

The woman in red joined the audience. She sat in the back of the auditorium because she felt less trapped there. The first miracle was that Sarah opened her mouth wide and sang with the rest of the chorus. The second miracle was that Sarah sang her solo beautifully. This time it was Max who cried because she was so happy for her daughter.

ASPERGER'S

1996, Age 34 –Now: At age 34, Max found herself in the waiting room of her dentist's office. She had a broken tooth that needed to be capped. After a while she tired of watching the giant fish tank. The woman in red picked up an old copy of *People* magazine and flipped through it. She stopped on an article about Temple Grandin. Temple Grandin was a woman with high functioning autism, or Asperger's Syndrome. As Max read about Temple's autistic traits, she realized that she had similar symptoms. For one, she had a hard time looking people in the eye. Initial touch bothered her, although deeper touch was okay. She thought in pictures instead of words. Many social situations, especially ones with small talk, were a puzzle to the woman in red. She experienced sensory overload in crowds and grocery stores. Her speech was delayed. Max thought, *I have high functioning autism, or Asperger's Syndrome!* She smiled deep inside herself. All of a sudden life made sense.

After she received her temporary crown, she snatched up the magazine and drove to the mama's house. The woman in red told her mother what she had discovered. The mama cried for joy. "Finally, we have name for it!"

A name for it meant Max didn't feel like she was going crazy. A name for it meant Macy wasn't so angry at the woman in red for pulling away from her touch. The nerdy woman admitted that she sometimes thought of leaving the relationship since she thought Max was pulling away physically because of emotional reasons. To find out that it was neurological, that initial touch really did feel like actual burning and pinching, that there was an explanation behind it, that gave Macy hope. The woman in red would improve on giving and receiving hugs because with therapy, she began to realize that people she loved weren't trying to harm her with their touch. It was her over sensitive nervous system that was causing the problem. Still, Max did not become a big hugger. The nerdy woman quit counting what was lost and started loving the few times Max snuggled up to her. The woman in red was no longer ashamed of being "shy" when others hugged easily. The couple could also make more sense of why Max wanted to remain in separate bedrooms. She needed the quiet even more than the usual introvert. The senses of the woman in red were turned on high, and she needed absolute quiet to be able to go to sleep.

Max had to find others like herself. She did a search on the internet, and she found Milan Dirksens. Milan Dirksens lived in the Netherlands. He started an internet list for autistic people and their families. On the list, the woman in red started writing Little Girl in Red stories about her childhood on the autistic spectrum. This attracted an audience of supporters from around the world. But Max felt lost on Milan's big list because it had so many people. So Milan started a smaller list for the woman in red and her friends. They named it Redrock Cave. In the virtual cave, Max wrote stories about her childhood and also about her days on the Alzheimer's unit when she was a chaplain. Both avenues would lead to books.

Around the same time, the woman in red joined a local Asperger's support group. Max explained to Billy, a psychologist and the leader of the group, that her autistic brain enjoyed one-on-one connections with people but had a difficult time being together with more than one of her kind in the group. The connection with the support group led to many speaking engagements including a theater production at Charlotte, NC. The speaking engagements usually included a reading of a Little Girl in Red story and were very cathartic. It felt so good to say it out loud. "I have Asperger's!" The support group came to an end a few years later when Billy, the leader, decided to live in Alabama full time.

Around the age of 45, Max got an official diagnosis of Asperger's Syndrome from the Autism Research Center to help her with her disability case. It verified what she already had discovered about herself in the twelve years since she read about Temple Grandin.

In those twelve years, the woman in red learned that the autistic spectrum was like a cafeteria line. The food represented the different autistic symptoms. Although there were a lot of people in line, different people had different things to eat. Most people on Milan's list were like

Max's brother. (Peter, aka My Boy, is undiagnosed, but he has some of the cafeteria line symptoms. Everybody in Max's family has a few symptoms. But the woman in red has the fullest plate in her family with the most symptoms.) Like Peter, the "aspies" on Milan's email list talked a lot about themselves and their special interests, and have since childhood. Max and a few others spoke very little as children, and only when they got older (college age for Max) did they start talking in monologues about themselves.

The woman in red found other autistics with delayed sex drives. It made her feel less retarded in that area. She and the others were angry for missing out on a big part of being a teenager. She also found others with literal minds that couldn't handle scary movies or Halloween. It wasn't that Max and the others were emotionally immature. Their brains had a difficult time reading the imaginary world that neuro-typicals (what autistics call everybody else, aka NTs) took for granted. The imaginary world felt very real to the woman in red and some of her new friends.

Max understood better why her body time clock didn't correspond to her soccer team's game starting times. It came naturally for her to go into herself and be in her own world than to be a part of the world around her. Macy had the family meal ready at six every evening. She said it was important to be consistent. The woman in red had a hard time understanding why she should eat when she wasn't starving. That is when she ate breakfast and sometimes lunch. She also had a hard time eating with others. Every little sound hurt her ears. And whatever the signal was for others that said the stomach was full, did not register with Max. She ate too much and didn't know when to stop.

The woman in red understood why it was easier to stay in contact with her church via email rather than being in the large congregation. Her senses got overloaded in a crowd. She felt every breath taken by the people around her. This was also why she had such a hard time going to Sarah's concerts. Max felt best in the back near the door where she felt like she could escape if necessary.

The woman in red dressed for comfort, not for fashion. She felt different from other females, in this concern. Macy was lesbian, but it didn't stop her from loving to dress up with her androgynous look. Even though the nerdy woman didn't wear make-up, she took extra care with her hair. Max barely looked at herself. She wasn't even sure that was her looking back in the mirror. She liked to wear red (and blue and black sometimes), and she liked to wear cotton. Even today, it takes her hardly any time to get ready in the morning. It was a relief to find other autistics similar in this area.

Max found it easier to be with cats and copy machines than with humans. She didn't have to make eye contact or talk. She felt like she was her most honest and favorite self with machines and animals. She also liked to be quiet with Macy. The woman in red liked to read in the same room as her lover. But these times were rare because Max had a difficult time reading the glaring words. She got a headache when she read the black ink on the white page. Sitting in rocking chairs on a porch in the mountains was another way to be close to the nerdy woman in the quiet. The woman in red preferred the shade to sunlight because her eyes hurt after a while, whether the light was natural or from a bulb.

When Max did talk, she preferred one-on-one conversations to groups. She didn't get worn out so soon that way. The woman in red was a gifted speaker. She knew this from the feedback from her sermons and speaking engagements. It was a thrill to connect with an audience. But it took a toll on Max's body. After a speaking engagement, she had to go to her bedroom and sit in the dark and quiet, to detox from too much human contact. Pictures of the event swirled too quickly in her mind's eye. She felt like she was going crazy and sometimes banged her head on the wall, attempting to get rid of the flashbacks.

The woman in red always lived in a world of pictures. One side of her brain was racing with pictures. It was why she did so well in math, science, and reading comprehension. She saw pictures of the correct answers. But the vocabulary side of her brain was moving too slowly. Learning new words would always be a burden. That was why Max performed poorly on the A.P. English test. She just couldn't get her vocabulary comprehension to match her ability to see vivid pictures of a story line.

The woman in red also saw pictures in her sleep, in the form of nightmares and night terrors. She felt like she was dying when she awoke in the middle of the night screaming. As a child, she dreamed of monsters. As an adult, the monsters were humans trying to kill Max in her dreams. Eventually, she would take an anti-depressant and an anti-psychotic medicine so as not to be so frightened. The medicines calmed her down but did not take away the nightmares.

Sometimes Macy went on trips for work or pleasure without the woman in red. The nerdy woman would fall out of the picture that Max had in her mind's eye. Macy would draw a map of where she was going and explain what she would be doing at certain times. This would keep the nerdy woman alive in the woman in red's brain. Otherwise, Max would erase Macy and miss her as if she were dead.

The woman in red found out that some autistics have a difficult time doing activities that require lining up both sides of the body, such as playing a piano, swimming, and driving a car. Max could barely play the piano after four years of lessons, she didn't learn to swim on top of the water until she was an adult, and she didn't get a driver's license until she was 19.

After she learned that her nerves were hyper-sensitive to initial touch, the woman in red realized later that the exception to this was when she played sports. When playing sports, she became hypo-sensitive, so that bumps with people, the ground, or the ball didn't hurt. It was why she liked to play football with the boys long ago. For a short time, she felt connected to other humans, the earth, and the ball. She also felt this connection with flag football in college and soccer in adulthood.

(These days...Max is somewhere in the middle, between the folks looking for a cure for autism and those who claim they are just fine the way they are. She wishes her senses were turned down. She has found some relief now that she is on medicine. The glare on the page isn't so bad, and she can read so much more. The woman in red can look people in the eye more often, and she can sit at the table and not worry quite so much about sounds. But she still gets sensory overloaded in crowds, although it isn't so bad that she hits her head on the wall.)

HARVEY TARVEY

1997, Age 35: Harvey Blume, a freelance writer in Massachusetts, was doing research on autism, and Milan Dirksens let him join his listserv in a limited way.

Max was doing her own "research," or reflecting, on her life. She was looking at how her life had been impacted by being on the autistic spectrum. The woman in red started emailing her lengthy reflections to Harvey Tarvey (as she referred to him in her emails). Sometimes she wrote as much as three times a day. Harvey responded with brief notes every third or fourth day. Max did not let Harvey hide behind the keyboard. She read his book *Ota Benga: The Pygmy in the Zoo*. The woman in red asked the author probing questions that often hit home.

Eventually, Max hopped a plane to Boston and visited Harvey. Unlike his email persona, in person, Harvey talked at length about his latest research on whatever article he was writing for online magazines. The woman in red found that she enjoyed arguing or discussing passionately with Harvey when they disagreed on a topic of common interest. Macy did not like to argue. She was a quiet woman who was ruled by reason. She only argued when she was angry, and as time went by, she was rarely angry. So it was fun for Max to meet someone quite different from her partner. She only wished she could visit Harvey more often because Harvey went back to his more hidden self when the woman in red returned home, and they began to correspond on email once again. The woman in red did visit two more times over the next couple of years.

The last time Max visited Harvey, she had him read the manuscript of her book about her years as a chaplain on an Alzheimer's unit. He agreed to write the forward, and the woman in red was touched deeply by his kind words on the page.

Eventually, the woman in red moved on from her exploration of Asperger's, and she slowly quit writing to Harvey so much. These days, they write each other every once in a while and are friends on Facebook. Max holds a special place in her heart for Harvey, who let her write all those words in all those emails over several years' time.

ALZHEIMER'S UNIT

August 1997-February 2003, Ages 35-41: Max started Clinical Pastoral Education (CPE) with the University Hospitals. In other words, she was a chaplain in training. Her day job was on the Alzheimer's unit. Once a week at night, she could be anywhere in the hospital system, being called to the room of any death. The woman in red loved her day job on the Alzheimer's unit. Persons with dementia were going where she had been with Asperger's as a child. Persons with Alzheimer's Disease looked at the floor instead of in the eye, and they had trouble with language. Max felt at home on the Alzheimer's unit.

While other professionals were counting losses, the woman in red kept finding spiritual connections with her patients. There was Ronny, who thought Max was the first woman preacher at his home church in the western part of the state. There was no convincing him that they were really in Charlotte, NC. There was also the woman who could still remember the hymns from way back when. She could barely talk, but, oh, boy, could she sing! There were the two women, one who spoke in scrambled sentences, the other who said nothing all day. One day, both women prayed in complete unscrambled sentences. It went on and on. The Alzheimer's unit was a gold mine for the woman in red. Like everybody else, she went in not expecting much but found that there was still a lot left to the people most of society had given up on. It was a matter of figuring out what was the disease versus an individual's core personality and his/her spirituality that was still there in most patients.

She was awarded the E. Malone Dodson Pastoral Care Fellowship in recognition of outstanding learning in pastoral care of persons with Alzheimer's Disease. When Max started telling her supervisor, Wilson Simons, all that she was discovering about persons with dementia, he told her to write it all down. Soon she had enough for a book. In 2002, the woman in red published her book about Alzheimer's spirituality. The book led to a successful speaking career about Alzheimer's spirituality. Max's chaplaincy with Elwood University Hospitals came to an end after five and a half years.

Unfortunately, Alzheimer's always ends in death. The woman in red would fall in love with her patients and then lose them. Max saw too much death. One death in particular she will never forget. Before Rachel died, the elderly woman saw Jesus in the sky, calling to her. She asked the woman in red if she could see him, too. This and over a hundred deaths from the Alzheimer's unit, plus night duty, were too close to the other side of reality. Max needed to get off the unit and into life. The people who had brought her the most joy when they were alive also brought her great sorrow when they died.

During this time three people who did not have dementia made a big difference to Max the years she worked on the Alzheimer's Unit. The afore mentioned Wilson Simons was the first. He taught the woman in red steadfastness by the example he led. Wilson followed Max on her Alzheimer's Unit journey from day one to the last day of work. He experienced with her the complete joy of being on the Alzheimer's Unit and also the downs of working with a population that eventually dies. Wilson also introduced his student to many speaking engagements. Wilson metaphorically held the hand of the woman in red until she was able to go on ahead without him.

Flora Holms was the second of these three influences. She literally worked right next door at the State's Alzheimer's Association. Flora was in charge of programming for the Association. When she saw that the woman in red had a talent for telling stories with meaning about her patients, Flora found her even more speaking engagements. One time Max and Flora were sharing a hotel room at one of the conferences of which they were both a part. Flora said she wanted the lights out, even though the woman in red was not finished with her speech for the next day. So Max went in the bathroom, shut the door, and wrote from the dry bathtub. Flora always thought that made a good story. Flora continued to meet with the woman in red even after she left the Alzheimer's unit. She was both funny and serious, which made her fun to be around.

Marie Logan was the third person that influenced Max. Marie, like Wilson, was a CPE supervisor. She also was a good copyeditor for both content and grammar. When Max thought she could never write an entire book, Marie urged her on. The two women met every week for a year to bring the book of the woman in red up to snuff. Marie believed in a book before Max saw the reality.

LAVENDER HILL BAPTIST CHURCH

1998, Age 36, The ordination process began. / 2004, Age 43, The ordination took place.: Lavender Hill Baptist Church which is in a Charlotte, NC. suburb, accepted African Americans into their congregation when most white churches moved north and east, away from the integrated, in-town neighborhoods. It was a stand that would cost them numbers, because a good portion of the congregation did not stay. Years later, the Baptist Church would stand up for gays and lesbians. For this, the Southern Baptist Convention broke relations with them.

Max joined the church sometime between the civil rights and sexuality issues. It was a great place to be accepted, when most churches didn't want to include her and Macy as a couple.

Some members of the church started an e-mail list, so the folks could quickly get information to each other. The woman in red loved the list. It was a way for her to share herself without being in a crowd. Going to the church services was a lot more difficult because Max experienced sensory overload. For years, the woman in red participated more on the email list than in the church building. It was Max's way to be a church member.

Lavender Hill Baptist Church was also the place to begin the process of ordination. In order to be hired at most places as a hospital or hospice chaplain, the woman in red needed to be ordained by her church and endorsed by her denomination. The process was frightening to Max because she had a hard time being a part of any group. Ordination made her face the fact that not only was she a part of a church, she cared for the people there, and they cared about her. The woman in red realized she was not alone in her ministry to Alzheimer's patients. There was a congregation who believed in her good work. So Max was ordained by her local church, but her ministry came to an end before she pursued the endorsement process with her denomination.

To this day, Lavender Hill Baptist Church is a loving and affirming place for the woman in red. She is active on the email list, and she attends the church services as often as her nervous system will allow her.

INFECTION

Fall of 1998, Age 37: After twenty years, the anterior cruciate ligament repair on Max's right knee wore out. Her knee joint started to move in and out of the socket. Her insurance did not give Dr. Meyer as a choice. Instead, she ended up with Dr. Folly, who was very cautious. He had no plans to stabilize the joint. He wanted to clean out the scar tissue and other imperfections. It was minor surgery with little risk. The woman in red healed quickly.

But five days after the surgery, her knee swelled and turned red. It became so painful that she went to the emergency room. The doctor at the emergency room called Dr. Folly, who arrived at 3 a.m. He pulled infection out of Max's knee with a big syringe. He looked the woman in red in the eye, "As soon as I get a team together, we're going to surgery. I have to clean out that joint." A few hours later, Max was waking up from a very painful surgery. All knee surgeries are painful, but the medicine used to combat the infection really hurt and made the woman in red weak. Max cried a lot and told Macy she couldn't take it another day. After two weeks, she was able to return to work.

The woman in red changed insurance and went to see Dr. Meyer. He knew other doctors were cautious with old injuries, but he was willing to attempt to fix the joint with a cadaver tendon. It worked until age 54. At age 54 Max got an artificial joint. Again Dr. Meyer was the surgeon.

GRAY

Spring 1999, Age 38: Max went to a pet store to buy fish. On the way to the fish section of the store, the woman in red passed a half grown Siamese kitten. The kitten spoke to Max, who knew Siamese because she had lived with Dilly the Siamese cat for the first 17 years of her life. The Siamese kitten in the pet store stated emphatically that she was ready to go home with the woman in red.

Max said, "I have to get the $100 first. That is how much you cost."

The kitten didn't understand. She wanted to go right then. The woman in red got paid the next day, so she said she would pay back a friend if the friend would lend the money immediately. Soon, the kitten said she was so happy to be leaving the store and finally going home.

At the time, Macy was in the mountains backpacking. Usually, Macy and Max made major decisions together. It was unlike the woman in red to make an impulsive purchase. But the kitten had talked to Max's soul. It was a very rare connection from the beginning. The woman in red worried that Macy would be mad about Gray. She had named the kitten for her beautiful fur. When Macy came home, Gray snuggled up to her like they were long lost friends. Macy was smitten. In fact, she fell so in love with Gray, she said if she and Max ever split up, then she (Macy) would take Gray with her. Gray was a smart cat. She treated each woman as if she was Gray's favorite. Interestingly, she scolded the children as if they were her bad kittens.

Gray loved to play fetch when she was young. Just as soon as the woman in red was falling asleep at night, Gray would drop a paper wad on Max's face. She would meow until the woman in red threw the wad. Max would try to go to sleep, just to have the paper wad land in her face again. Gray did not try this trick on Macy, only the woman in red. Even now in her old age, Gray likes to pull a tape measure around the house. She meows for Max to play, too. Gray is a rare cat. She will come when she is called. She also comes when the woman in red cries. Best of all, Gray helped the woman in red with touch. Blue loves to be petted, and she will not take "no" for an answer. She likes to snuggle close to her human.

When Gray was a year old, Peter, Max's brother, said he wanted Gray's kitten. He found a suitor for Gray and arranged the mating ritual. Gray gave birth to four healthy kittens. At first, she howled whenever the woman in red tried to leave her side. She did not want to be left alone with those little furry aliens. Eventually, she would let Max out of the room. Peter took two kittens. Sasha, his wife, is eternally grateful. The woman in red kept a sweet loving girl named Hershey, but Gray picked on the younger cat. So Max's mother took Hershey, and the human mama and Gray's daughter have been friends ever since.

These days when Max comes home, Gray tells her everything that has happened while she was gone. When family or friends come over, Gray tells all of the secrets of the woman in red.

Max is pretty sure that Gray is taking a vacation from her usual job as empress of the universe. She is resting in a cat's body, but every once in a while, Gray gets a far away look in her eyes. That is when the woman in red figures Gray is dictating orders to her subordinates. Blue knows that the Max has figured all this out and expects to be treated as the royalty that she is.

Sometime in the future Gray will die, and the woman in red will mourn and howl because she has never known such a deep connection with an animal.

BAD PICTURES

Summer 1999, Age 37: Max started to see vivid pictures inside her head of herself committing suicide. The woman in red saw herself hanging from the porch railing, cutting her wrists, drowning in the bathtub, or shooting herself in the head. The pictures were so real and frequent, she couldn't just ignore them. Max had seen over a hundred deaths as a hospital chaplain. Death was in her pores. She was diagnosed with depression and anxiety.

The woman in red did not want to start on medication, but she had no choice if she wanted help with the bad pictures. Max began taking an anti-depressant and an anti-psychotic. The prescribed drugs did not erase the pictures, but they kept the woman in red calm. They also helped with night terrors. She didn't scream out at night so much. The medications toned down Max's senses. She could tolerate touch more, and sounds did not drive her as crazy, as before. Best of all, she could read without the glare on the page hurting her eyes.

A few months after the woman in red began the medications, Macy was watching N.C. baseball. She was stretched out on the sofa futon.

Max climbed up on the futon next to her nerdy woman and tried to get into the game. She was a sometimes fan, especially when the team did well. Macy, on the other hand, was an avid fan.

The nerdy woman continued to look at the television screen when she said, "I'm scared."

"Of what?" the woman in red looked over at Macy, who finally looked back at Max.

"That you will do what the pictures tell you to do, that you will commit suicide. I have been trying to be strong for you, but I don't feel strong."

"I don't need you to be strong for me. I don't need you to take care of me, even though I know a lot of folks think that is what you do for me. I just need you to be honest, like you are now."

"If you try to commit suicide, I will be so mad at you."

"I have no plans to commit suicide. I read a book in college called *Return From Tomorrow,* by George C. Ritchie. It was about a man who died and came back to life. While he was dead, he met Jesus. Before he met Jesus, he saw all kinds of things, including dead people who were begging forgiveness from living people who could not hear the dead people. He realized that the dead people were the folks who had committed suicide. I don't want to be one of those people, spending I don't know how long, begging you to forgive me. Besides, I don't want to make you feel immense pain. I especially think of Zeb and Sarah. I don't want to cause them the pain of having a mother who commits suicide. If I feel like I am getting close to committing suicide, I will go to the mental hospital first. I promise."

"You promise?"

"Yes. I do not feel that I am anywhere near suicide today."

"Good. I love you." A tear fell from the nerdy woman's eye.

"I know," the woman in red smirked.

"Damn you! Don't you tease me right now."

"I love you," Max affirmed.

Macy put her hand on the knee of woman in red. "You are my woman. Do not hurt my woman."

"Yes, Ma'am."

JAPAN

February 2000, Age 38: Max's sister, Lila, lived in Japan, in a town in the southern part of the country. Lila taught English and was a Christian missionary. She and her husband Hugo adopted two-year-old Matma from India, right after they gave birth to Baby June. Baby June was named for Aunt June. It was a chaotic time in their household. The mama and Max volunteered to go to Japan and help for two weeks.

The flight over was thirteen hours. After six hours on the plane, the woman in red thought she was going to go crazy because she had seven hours to go. The mama used fingernail polish remover to clean her fingernails on the plane. She was putting the polish back on when a stewardess said the mama couldn't do that because they were all breathing the same recycled air. The fumes were too much.

The mama said, "But I've only got two more to go."

The stewardess looked confused by the mama's response.

The woman in red giggled to herself. The mama was funny.

Japan was like another planet, not just another country. Everybody wore dark blue, black, brown, and gray jackets. Max was wearing a bright yellow parka. She felt like a neon sign.

Like most people in their Japanese town, Lila and Hugo did not run the heat at night. The woman in red had to wear a stocking hat and pile on the covers. She could see her breath in the morning. Lila paid for the luxury of a heated toilet seat. It made sense in a cold house.

June was a delightful baby who cooed and smiled at Max. She reminded the woman in red of Zeb when he was a baby. Little Matma was miserable because she missed the nuns who had kept her to age two. She cried a lot.

One day, the mama and Lila went sightseeing. Hugo sent Max to the grocery store by herself to get eggs and a few other items. The woman in red did not know the language, so she was a bit intimidated. When Max checked out at the register, the wrong price came up for the eggs. The cashier panicked and called over her co-workers. The four Japanese women met in a huddle. Finally, one said in English to the woman in red, "Wrong price. We fix."

"Okay," said Max.

When she got home to Hugo the woman in red said, "I really upset the grocers."

Hugo explained that some Japanese thought Americans were going to blow their stacks, like the bombs we dropped in World War II.

Max liked helping Lila and Hugo, but it was time to go home to Macy, Zeb, and Sarah. She slept from exhaustion the whole flight home.

Six and half years later, Hugo, Lila, Matma, June, and baby Eliza arrived in the U.S.A. for good. They moved in with the mama.

ZEB AND ROTC

Fall 2000-Spring 2004, Ages 39-42: When Zeb was in fifth grade, he didn't move on the soccer field, and he wouldn't play in chess tournaments. He was gifted in both areas, but he was frozen. When Max grilled him about why he just stood on the soccer field, Zeb said the wolverines were trying to eat the bunnies, and the bunnies weren't safe. The woman in red looked at Macy with a worried look. She sent Zeb to psychotherapy with Riley, who had helped Sarah years earlier. After a few months, Zeb said to his mom, "You are just going to have to accept me the way I am." Max accepted that Zeb would not return to soccer or chess club. She made him continue to play his violin. In the two areas in which he was gifted, he felt pressure and quit. In the area he was good enough, he continued. It was heartbreaking for a mother to watch.

In ninth grade, Zeb found the extra-curricular activity that fit him. He joined Jr. Navy ROTC to get all the medals and ribbons. It was a fun game to him. In order to get the academic award, he had to pull up his grades to A's. He joined the Jr. Navy ROTC rifle team and did very well. For the next three years, Zeb got a lot of medals and ribbons.

The teacher called Commander thought Zeb should be in the top student slot his senior year. Zeb refused it and the second position, too. In fact, he wanted to quit. The woman in red said he would have to return to soccer if he quit. Zeb decided ROTC was the lesser of the two evils. He accepted the third slot and was in charge of field trips. He decided that Jr. Navy ROTC should go to Hawaii for spring break. Commander said they had to go to a different military landmark each day. Zeb said that then they had to go to a different beach each afternoon. The trip was a huge success.

As part of his position as number three in charge, Zeb emceed the ROTC awards banquet at the end of the year. He was very funny and held the audience's attention. Zeb also wrote and read an essay about what Jr. Navy ROTC had meant to him. He made his mother cry.

After high school, Zeb enlisted in the Marines. He became an air traffic controller.

SARAH AND THE VIOLA

Fall 2001-Spring 2005, Ages 40-45: Sarah could feel music in her soul. When she and Zeb played duets on her viola and his violin, Sarah would change the notes to what she thought sounded better. This drove Zeb crazy because he followed the notes on the page. Zeb and Sarah played for the patients on Max's Alzheimer's unit. The dementia patients loved the children. Part of the reason they were so good was because the woman in red was a strict mother who made her children practice their instruments almost every week day.

After junior high, Zeb gave up the violin, but Sarah continued with her high school orchestra, the county honor orchestra, and also the metro counties symphony orchestra in eleventh and twelfth grades. The metro counties conductor became Sarah's private instructor. She insisted on the need to know advanced technique. Sarah left her lessons in tears and claimed, "She hates me." But she was becoming a better violist. She even made the third seat for the metro counties her senior year. It was a big deal because she was with the best of the best from all over Charlotte, NC. Sarah made the county orchestra in eighth grade because she was so talented and worked so hard. She remained in the county orchestra throughout high school and went to China with them to perform all over Beijing and to see The Great Wall and The Forbidden City. In her senior year, Sarah was first chair in the county orchestra. Sarah was also first chair in both her junior and senior high school symphonies every year. Unfortunately Sarah injured her shoulder from the weight of the viola and the long practices. This would influence the future of Sarah and the viola.

Max's daughter decided to study viola. But it went from her major to minor when yet again her shoulder hurt. Sarah's major became political science, with a concentration in pre-law and a minor in music. The orchestra concerts of which Sarah was a part were spectacular, and the woman in red was so proud of her daughter.

These days Sarah plays viola with her husband Kevin, while he plays guitar in the privacy of their home. Someday, she hopes to join an ensemble or a small orchestra and/or teach viola.

TALKING KNIVES

December 2004, Age 43: "You need to come home." The woman in red said into the phone.

Twenty minutes later, Macy found Max in a ball on the kitchen floor. "What happened?"

"The knives floated out of the drawer and said they were going to cut my wrists. They said I won't be able to get away from them."

At the emergency room, the woman in red paced the floor and shivered with fear. She was sure she had had a psychotic break. She signed the papers to commit herself onto the psych unit. Max howled in despair when Macy had to leave. The woman in red felt a chill of intense loneliness. She couldn't go home because the knives would get her, but she didn't want to be locked up.

The doctor was extremely kind and understanding. He diagnosed Max with major depressive disorder with psychotic features. Not only would he increase the medications the woman in red was already taking, the doctor would also add two other drugs. Max would be over medicated for the next two years. It was a necessary evil to keep the knives from floating out of the drawer. The next year would mean another trip to the hospital because the suicidal pictures she had been seeing became too frequent.

The talking knives and too frequent suicidal pictures occurred after Zeb joined the Marines. The day Zeb graduated from bootcamp, Max watched her sweet, loving child march like a military robot. It broke her heart. Zeb announced that he was going to war. The anticipation brought the woman in red over the edge. But when Zeb really did go to war, the woman in red felt a grace that protected her heart. It was only in the anticipation stage that she made herself crazy.

Max would have to take out most of the stress from her life. Today it has been thirteen years since the knives floated out of the drawer, and the suicidal pictures have mostly stopped. Every once in a while the suicidal pictures creep up on her when she feels too much stress. The woman in red is now on four medications, Citalopram (Celexa), Abilify,

Prazocin, and Risperidone, but she is not overmedicated. The medications don't stop the suicidal pictures completely, lack of stress does that. The medications keeps the woman in red calm when the bad pictures and night terrors come. But they don't come as often now that she is on this combination of medications.

GRAND CANYON

Spring 2005/Spring 2006, Ages 43 and 44: When Macy turned fifty, she decided that she and Max would visit the Grand Canyon. They had been together fifteen years. The trip was marvelous! They stood at the rim and watched birds of prey swoop in and out of the canyon. They took hikes and breathed in the fresh air. And they sat in the quiet of their cabin and read all about the history of the land. So Macy said, "Let's go again next year." That was what they did.

The second year, they first went to a National Park in southern Utah. Zion had incredible red rock formations that made the woman in red's heart sing. She wished they could live right next to the park.

When they slept in the lodge right next to the Grand Canyon that second year, Max heard the canyon call to her to come and play. She felt a force pulling her to jump in the canyon. It was similar to the knives coming out of the drawer and talking to her. The woman in red decided she would never sleep that close to a canyon again.

The best part of the whole trip was a one-day raft trip down the Colorado River inside the canyon. They got splashed by the freezing cold water and looked up at the sheer cliffs. At the end of the raft trip, the women were flown out by helicopter. The helicopter turned sideways and Max could see the river from way up high. It was thrilling. The woman in red was thankful that Macy insisted on seeing the Grand Canyon two years in a row.

CANCER

2007-2008, Ages 45-46: In April 2007, a CAT scan showed a tumor the size of a football in Macy's abdomen. She was 52. She and Max had been together seventeen and a half years. The tumor was attached to the nerdy woman's pancreas and liver. The liver function was blocked. A stent was put in to get the liver working, and a biopsy was taken. The biopsy showed non-Hodgkins Lymphoma. It was a more curable cancer than the alternative, liver cancer. Macy held her own through radiation and chemo. She was able to work part-time as a Clinical Pastoral Education (CPE) supervisor. She taught hospital chaplains. Macy loved her work, and she loved Max, Zeb, and Sarah. She also still loved to learn and was part of a training for CPE supervisors and therapists. Macy was still Max's nerdy woman. The nerdy woman refused to consider death as an option. When the chemo treatments were over, Macy went to England with her training program for a week. She brought back a rugby shirt to the woman in red. Max felt death looming, but the nerdy woman refused to talk about it, except she did share a dream. Macy's dead parents appeared in the dream and said their daughter would be joining them soon.

The radiation and chemo shrunk the tumor some but didn't get rid of the lymphoma. The nerdy woman needed a stem cell transplant almost a year after she had been diagnosed with cancer. Her brother Bob was a match. The transplant was just two bags of platelets draining into Macy's arm. It was anti-climatic. A few days later, a high fever put her in the hospital. A few days after that, the nerdy woman had a brain bleed in a part of the brain that could not be drained, and she fell into a coma. After a couple of weeks and a probable stroke, the doctors said Macy was not going to get any better or wake up. Max gave the okay to take the nerdy woman off of life support. A few weeks later, Macy was dead. Max felt strong all through the nerdy woman's illness. She felt the least amount of depression and anxiety she had known in years.

But after the memorial service, the woman in red didn't want to get out of bed. The mama called every day and said, "Get up! We're going to lunch." Aunt Lydia also took Max to lunch every Wednesday. Just getting from hour to hour was painful. The woman in red would watch movies with her brother-in-law Hugo, while Lila went to law school. The daddy bought her groceries on the weekends. Many friends took her to eat and helped her clean out Macy's possessions and do her finances. Max saw Jean once a week in therapy. She participated in a grief group and went to church every single Sunday (for the first time since her marriage). She desperately needed to be around people. The woman in red preferred the sensory overload, that bothered her, to being alone in her grief.

Gray, the cat howled in the middle of the living room every night for months. She and the woman in red just wanted Macy to come back. The mama and Aunt Lydia kept calling. Max continued therapy, even though some days it felt like she was getting nowhere. Very slowly, the woman in red got better, and she learned to live without Macy. As of this writing, it has been nine years since her partner's death. Max rarely thinks about her nerdy woman anymore. But when she does, it is with great fondness.

FINDING MEANING

So what do we make of a life that has been tossed through storms that the woman in red wouldn't wish on another? The biggest thing she has learned from it all is that she can open her heart to others. Her childhood was lonely because she barely talked, and she let very few people hug her. The monsters visited her every night and sometimes in the day, too. Today, Max thinks the monsters came from not getting her parents' protection that she would have received if she had talked to her parents and accepted their hugs. When a person is trapped inside herself, she can't always tell the difference between what is imagined and what is real. The monsters felt very real throughout her childhood. Loneliness is a powerful thing.

But all was not lonely. Max had many people love her, even though she kept her distance. Aunt Lydia, Aunt June, and Uncle Oscar made a lasting impact of love and acceptance. Aunts and uncles aren't as critical as mothers and fathers. They don't worry so much about being normal. Max has now experienced that from the other side of being both a mother and an aunt. Aunt and uncles are more likely to accept nieces and nephews for who they are. There is enough distance there to not need to judge so much.

Amy and Caroline were a big influence on Max. They protected her from being ridiculed because she didn't wear the right clothes and didn't say much. The fact that they liked the little girl in red, the medium girl in maroon, and the girl in beige helped fight away the loneliness and the monsters that came with living inside herself.

The girl in beige's high school teachers helped with self-esteem, especially Coach Rizzo -- the chemistry teacher, Ms. Logic -- the math teacher, and Ms. Leadman -- the English teacher. They made Max want to get up and go to school.

The young woman in Blue made it through life because of her relationships with Mason -- her husband and her friend, Cassie -- the kind young woman who listened so well, Ray -- the Bible study buddy who made studying fun, Caroline (before she died) -- her childhood friend who still believed in Max, Derek Hayes -- her undergrad philosophy professor who made Max think she could do anything, Grayson Donaldson -- her seminary professor who made class fun and interesting, and Sheila -- her therapist who helped to stop the monsters. Max felt close to Jesus during those years. She truly believed that Jesus would not mislead her. She poured out her heart to him, and miracles happened around her.

The woman in red will always remember Macy -- her lover, best friend, and partner. She is also thankful for Jean -- her therapist that she still has today. Jean has helped to fight the depression and suicidal pictures more than anybody else. She is so positive that she tricks Max into thinking it is going to be a great day, when the depression is saying it isn't. These days, the mama still calls Max every day for lunch. It has taken years of therapy to finally let the mama into the heart of the woman in red. Like most children, Max blamed her mother for her years of pain. But her grownup self has learned that the mama is human like everybody else. She is both good and bad, and right now the good outweighs the bad.

The woman in red found her best work as a chaplain on the Alzheimer's unit. She danced and laughed and prayed with her patients. But she also cried when each one of them died. What brought her life also brought her death.

The suicidal pictures still haunt Max every once in a while when Zeb moved to D.C. from NC, and the pictures came back. Both an increase in medicine and talking about the pictures with Jean, her therapist, helped them go away.

The woman in red prefers the quiet corners of the universe, like her computer screen where she writes. But she needs human contact just like everybody else. It isn't enough to read, write, and snuggle with the kitties. So she ventures past her autistic skin and connects with other humans. It is a balance, between quiet and connection, she will always need to maintain.

THESE DAYS

These days, the woman in red goes to water aerobics at the YMCA in the mornings at least two times a week. There is a deep water class at 9:00 a.m. and a shallow water class at 10:00 a.m. She attends both classes and also tries to swim some laps.

For four years, Max visited with her three nieces (My Baby's aka Lila's children), Matma, June, and Eliza in the afternoons. In the summer, they went swimming at the local pool. They also loved going to the zoo together, visiting the library, listening to Beatles' tunes, and buying frozen drinks.

Max still sees Jean in therapy and still goes to church at Lavender Hill Baptist Church. She also continues to participate on the Lavender Hill email listserv. She writes a blog type message on the listserv about twice a week. The woman in red has participated four times in her church's Arts Café. She reads portions of this memoir. She has also hosted the Arts Café. Max also had a speaking engagement with the mama's teachers' union about Alzheimer's Spirituality.

Gray the cat has been joined by younger boy Siamese cat named Cloudy. Cloudy is a rascal monkey who gets into everything. Gray still talks a lot and makes Max feel welcome on this planet. Since the fall of 2013 Max has lived in the basement apartment of the mama's house. She, Gray and Cloudy are content there.

Zeb left the Marines with an honorable discharge. He went to an Aeronautical University and studied Aeronautics, with a minor in management. He graduated Suma Cum Laude. Now he works for Immigration and Citizenship. He is married to Brenda who is a good match for his dry wit. They moved to Oregon to be near Brenda's family business.

Sarah finished UNC in the top 10% of her class. She worked for an Airlines in Oregon, for many years. She and her husband, Kevin lived in the NYC area before moving back to Oregon. They are good together and now have a baby girl.

My Boy, Peter, is a Kroger store manager. He lives with his lovely wife Sasha. For 17 years they had two of Gray's kittens. Now they are trying to decide when they will get new kittens.

My Baby, Lila, loved being a public defender. Her husband Hugo died in 2010 of complications from his muscular dystrophy. Lila is remarried to Mike, and they lived in a large house in metro Charlotte,

NC with their three girls for a year. They have moved to the North Carolina Mountains where Lila started her own legal practice. Lila now works for the D.A. in her area. Max now sees her nieces on holidays.

The daddy also died in 2010. Although his death was related to his years of drinking, he was not drinking when he died.

Mason, Max's ex-husband, is remarried and keeps in touch with Zeb and Sarah. He has been a good father for many years now. He is a lawyer and a pastor. He helped Max and the mama write their wills.

Amy, aka the smart girl when they were children, pulls together eight old high school buddies every few months. Max is one of them. The woman in red also likes to eat lunch with Amy and Amy's mother, Joanie. Joanie helped Max edit her first book, but now has dementia.

Cassie, aka the kind young woman, keeps in regular contact with Max via email. After many years of silence, Phelps, the college roommate, found the woman in red on Facebook in 2014. It was a joyous reunion with a lot of catching up to do.

Liz Waller, aka the step-mother, and Max ran into each other at a coffee shop fifteen years ago. They were very happy to see each other. Ms. Waller said the woman in red should write a play about their year together and Ms. Waller would direct it.

Cousins Penny, Amanda, Sheldon, and Jason live in South Carolina with their families. Cousin Ada Lynn lives in Montana with her husband. Max is friends with them all on Facebook. Aunt June passed away in 2016.

Aunt Lydia lived in the southern part of Charlotte, NC and ate lunch with Max and the mama two or three times a month from the time Macy died until recently. Aunt Lydia's daughter Reide lives Arizona with her husband. The woman in red drove her aunt to Arizona to live in a retirement community. They made many fun stops on the way including visiting Graceland. Max will miss her aunt very much. Cousin Dan lives with his wife in New York. Cousin Walt died an early death due to colon cancer.

Cousin Jeremy lives with his husband in Texas. Cousin T.J. unfortunately is in jail.

Because of going to therapy with Jean, remaining on her medications, eating lunches with the mama, going to water aerobics, and writing each day, Max is more at peace than ever before. She is learning to live with her Asperger's and depression with psychotic features. She knows Macy is happy for her.

Except on Rare Occasions

Tonight I have been remembering
Macy's feet.
They were skinny, pale things.
It was funny how she had that
China doll skin and such dainty looking feet,
but she had knocked one of her big toe nails
off over and over again from being so
aggressive playing soccer.
She was a mean soccer player,
would argue with the refs and get
a yellow card.
And that toenail as stubborn as the nerdy woman herself,
would grow back in an ugly yellow color,
a total contrast to those ultra feminine footsies.

I rarely think about Macy.
For so long it hurt too much.
I just got used to picking myself back up,
pushing ahead, forgetting all that was lost,
never lingering on what was,
refusing to let in the pure joy I knew with her.
No, life is to be trudged through now,
no more jumping in mud puddles.

But sitting here in the quiet,
with my electric fan blowing in my face,
I remembered her feet peeking out of the covers.
In the winter she wore thick wool socks to bed
because she had poor circulation.
I can't wear wool on my sensitive skin.
She had a drawer overflowing with
so many wool socks.
She couldn't seem to buy enough,
as if the more she bought,
the warmer her feet would be.

I remember when she got out of the hot hot shower
she would be pink.
That pale pale skin would pink up every time.
Her feet the pinkest of all with that ugly yellow nail.

Where do our bodies go after cremation?
Do we look like ourselves in heaven?
When I see Macy again
will she prove to me that it is really she
by pointing to the ugly nail?

She used to spoil me at Christmas,
spend too much on me.
let me pick out whatever I wanted.
We would get so excited about giving each other
presents that we couldn't wait until Christmas.
Late Christmas Eve,
after church,
after my mother's celebration,
barely able to keep our eyes open,
we would unwrap our gifts to each other.
It was a private affair.
We would celebrate the kids in the morning,
but our time was behind our closed door.
We always spent more than we should.
We were so frugal the rest of the year.
But late Christmas Eve was when we
celebrated each other, our love
that was better than
anything we had experienced before.

It would be the nerdy woman's last love.
I am sure one day I will find another.
When I imagine Macy these days,
I see her in heaven leading a band of women
to backpack in the woods, the wilderness.
It was a fantasy we spoke of often.
When are we going to get together a group of women
and go camping?

Which of all our favorite places should we take them?
But we were such introverts,
it was never realized.
So I think she is doing that now,
picking out the most innovative tent,
making sure her hiking boots fit.
She always had to wear two pairs of socks
because her feet were so thin.
I remember when she bought me my first
super duper sleeping bag our first year together.
I knew she loved me then.
She was always torn between her intellect,
that insisted on getting a Th.D.,
and her love of the outdoors.
I guess it is because her intellect got so much attention,
and we just didn't get to her beloved wilderness enough
that I think she is now showing
women around Eden.

I admit it.
I miss her,
and I want her back.
But she has taken a different path from me.
Macy is free,
and here I sit with all my neuroses
and psychotic features,
still stuck in my skin.

People always thought that she was the
strong one,
but as she pointed out,
we were equally strong and weak.
Most of her problems were kept secret,
unlike mine.
That is why folks thought she had it all together.
But I knew the truth.
I have never before felt so equally yoked.

Do you see me, Macy?
Or are you so involved with your next life
that you don't have time to look back?
I will go back to being busy,
never letting myself think of you
except on rare occasions like tonight.

Love,
Max